SMALL-SPACE
CONTAINER
GARDENS

SMALL-SPACE CONTAINER GARDENS

Transform Your
Balcony, Porch, or Patio
with Fruits, Flowers,
Foliage & Herbs

FERN RICHARDSON

TIMBER PRESS
Portland · London

Published in 2012
by Timber Press, Inc.

The Haseltine Building
133 S.W. Second Avenue,
Suite 450
Portland, Oregon
97204-3527
timberpress.com

2 The Quadrant
135 Salusbury Road
London NW6 6RJ
timberpress.co.uk

Design by Omnivore
Printed in China

Library of Congress Cataloging-
in-Publication Data
Richardson, Fern.
    Small-space container gardens:
transform your balcony, porch, or
patio with fruits, flowers, foliage
& herbs / Fern Richardson. —1st
edition.
        p. cm.
    Includes bibliographical
references and index.
    ISBN-13: 978-1-60469-241-9
1. Container gardening.
2. Small gardens.
I. Title.
SB418.R53 2012
635.9'86—dc23
                    2011029272

A catalog record for this
book is also available from
the British Library.

Contents

Foreword

By DEBRA LEE BALDWIN

THE APARTMENT FERN RICHARDSON shares with her husband has minimal outdoor space. Yet the busy career woman, avid gardener, and self-taught horticulturist cultivates whatever she likes and does it with style.

Fern's enthusiasm for container gardening and her success with growing plants that provide food, beauty, and bouquets have led her to share her small-space savvy with apartment and condo dwellers worldwide. No wonder her blog, *Life on the Balcony*, is so popular. Fern is fearless. I don't doubt that if she wanted to grow a wildflower meadow on a rooftop, she'd find a way. Fern—yes, that's really her name—grows jewel-like succulents, fragrant herbs, potted fruit trees, vegetables that change kaleidoscopically with the seasons, and flowering vines that serve as privacy screens.

If you don't like your outdoor living area and you wish you did—if you're uncertain where to start, what to plant, or how to keep it alive—you're about to embark on an exciting journey. What sets this

Fern Richardson's bountiful balcony.

book apart from others about container gardening is that its author is a space-saving maven. Fern sees walls, rafters, railings, and everything in-between as fair game. And she does it economically. If you're short on cash (or even if you're not), look forward to discovering how to start plants from seeds; take cuttings; and transform found objects, like wood pallets, into attractive vertical planters.

In order to have variety without clutter—after all, balconies are mainly for people—Fern extensively researches her plant selections. Just about everything she chooses does double- or triple-duty. Her fig tree, for example, is a dwarf variety ideally suited to container culture, has large leaves that stand out amid finer-textured foliage, and provides delicious fruit. Fern is also a naturalist who knows how to attract and nurture beneficial insects, like ladybugs and butterflies, while at the same time preventing infestations of ants, aphids, and mealy bugs—all without resorting to toxic chemicals. As she shoehorns an entire garden into a space no bigger than the average bathroom, Fern makes sure everything looks good. She explains how to primp your plants, and how to hide mundane yet essential items such as fertilizer, pruners, and bags of potting soil.

So if your entryway, patio, deck, balcony, or rooftop is a stark expanse populated only by beach chairs and a hibachi, take the plunge. Claim that space for your own private Eden. I'm betting that your yard-owning friends soon will envy you. Weed-pulling and lawn care—which consume the Saturdays of many a suburban homeowner—will not concern you. Yet you'll post photos of geometric succulents, hanging baskets, and drowsy butterflies; fill vases with bright blooms; and serve salads of home-grown lettuce and vine-ripened tomatoes.

Keep in mind that Fern may not have a yard, but she certainly has a garden. And thanks to this book, so will you.

DEBRA LEE BALDWIN *is the author of* Succulent Container Gardens *and* Designing with Succulents.

Preface

CONTAINER GARDENING ON BALCONIES, patios, porches, terraces, decks, rooftops, or even windowsills is a fun way for those of us without a "real" garden to still get our hands dirty. I find that gardening on my balcony satisfies my need to grow—herbs, peaches, nectarines, figs, blueberries, flowers, and succulents—while still leaving plenty of time and energy for other parts of my life. The space I've created, and the process of caring for it, is also my retreat. When my husband insists on practicing the same song on his guitar, over and over and over, I can easily escape to the relative peace and quiet of my balcony garden. Even though container gardens are inherently less wild than a traditional garden—they are, after all, contained—I love that it's still possible to be surrounded with lushness, beauty, nature, privacy, and style.

Connected so intimately to our indoor living areas, balconies, patios, and porches also serve as transitional spaces between inside and out that naturally invite personal touches and creativity. Many people love plants and keep adding to their collection, but feel frustrated that their balcony or

I always grow burro's tail (*Sedum morganianum*) because it was one of the plants my grandma gave me as a cutting from her garden.

11

patio doesn't reflect their unique style. That's where having a design strategy comes into play. In the first part of the book you'll learn how to make harmonious plant combinations and compositions, pick containers that are equally pleasing to plant and person, and utilize your space—on the floor, up the wall, over the railing—to its fullest potential. You'll get ideas on redefining what makes a container a container, incorporating decorative touches, and, above all, unleashing your personality.

Throughout the book you'll also find plenty of practical information that shows you how to deal with unique challenges, like the microclimate of a windy balcony or a patio that gets the brunt of every rain storm. The final two chapters give you a basic crash course in cultivating your container gardening green thumb, as well as troubleshooting some common pests and diseases.

The five design chapters include multitudes of plant picks and tips to help you attract birds and beneficial insects to your garden, simultaneously satiate your hunger and your discerning eye, create a secret garden hidden away from nearby neighbors and noises, assemble a pathway of stunning succulents and fragrant plants, or luxuriate in a tropically themed refuge. I've included simplified design plans which you can use as inspirational blueprints or as jumping off points to mix and match plants from one chapter to another. No matter how you decide to use this book, I hope it motivates you to head outside and create your own oasis. You won't regret it!

Small spaces require less work to keep them looking good. This low-maintenance patio garden was designed by Felix Navarro, owner of The Juicy Leaf in Venice, California.

SMALL AND SASSY

Choosing Colors, Containers, Furniture, and Lighting

PLANTS ARE WONDERFUL for creating lushness, providing privacy, and adding beauty to a small space, but it's the details—the containers that hold the flowers, the rug beneath your feet, the lantern on the table—that transform a space with plants into a true garden retreat. After all, it's much easier to enjoy the beauty of your plants when you're perched on a charming café chair and marveling at how everything looks in the twinkling light of candles.

Before you get going, it helps to familiarize yourself with the size of your space. Draw a rough sketch on grid paper and make a note of your measurements on the drawing. Photocopy or scan it into your computer so you can draw multiple layouts of pots, seating, tables, and more. You should also take a little time to think about your lifestyle and how you envision using your space: Do you want to grow your own food? Do you entertain a lot? Would you like to lie out on a chaise lounge and read a book? Let your desires guide your choices. Start browsing magazines, books, and garden websites to figure out the kinds of pots and plants that fit your style. Add notes and clippings to your balcony sketch.

The repetition of warm colors in the rug, cushions, and umbrella help this patio garden feel cozy and inviting.

No matter the layout of your space or the style that you're seeking, you can find ways to make it feel bigger, and of course, better.

Plant Color Schemes

Flowers and foliage can be found in every conceivable color, and the combination possibilities will push even active imaginations to their limit. In a small space, such as the typical balcony, formulating a color plan can help the garden look intentional and purposefully put together. A valuable tip for people who feel a bit paralyzed when it comes to making color choices is to go back to basics—a color wheel.

Simple monochromatic color schemes involve picking one color that you like and then limiting your plant choices to that color of flowers or foliage. Monochromatic doesn't have to be the exact same shade of any given color; it could mean shades of pink, from the lightest baby pink to the deepest magenta and everything in between. A good idea for all gardens, but especially monochromatic ones, is to choose plants that flower at different times throughout the season so there will always be something interesting to observe that establishes your theme. I find that monochromatic gardens often feel restful, peaceful, modern, or sophisticated.

The analogous color approach entails choosing two (or three) colors that are next to each other on the color wheel, like yellow and orange. I love this subtly sophisticated way of injecting color into a planting scheme. Selecting complementary colors, which are directly opposite each other on the color wheel, brings out the best in each color, making them both pop. For example, blue and orange both look brighter and peppier when paired with one another.

Additional schemes could be based on primary, secondary, or tertiary colors. In case it has been awhile since your last art class, primary colors—red, blue, yellow—are the basis of all other colors. Secondary colors—purple, orange, green—result from mixing two primary colors together. And tertiary colors are the combination of primary and secondary colors. These three color combinations tend to be the most intense and will appear bold or playful. Tone down the intensity level by mixing in white or cream plants. Or use muted, pastel versions of each color like lavender, apricot, and soft green instead of vibrant purple, bright orange, and lime green.

Use a color wheel to visualize enticing plant combinations.

MONOCHROMATIC

✳ Nothing is classier than a row of white roses in large Italian-style terracotta pots—bonus points if you underplant the roses with a white-and-green foliage plant, like variegated ivy.

✳ Imagine the drama of black bachelor's buttons, black calla lilies, and black sweet potato vine.

✳ Go for year-round purple: hyacinths for early spring, irises for late spring and early summer, statice for late summer into fall, and purple pansies to keep the color alive in winter.

ANALOGOUS

✳ Try a red cascade of petunias intermixed with orange calibrachoa; or red impatiens with a purple sweet potato vine.

✳ Purple snapdragons skirted by blue lobelia could be interesting; or blue angelonia as a nice contrast with the spiky green foliage of sweet flag.

✳ Lime green sweet potato foliage looks awesome with the lemony flowers of nemesia; or complement warm yellow African daisies with coppery carex.

COMPLEMENTARY

✳ A purple variety of coral bells sets off yellow-flowered marguerite daisies nicely.

✳ Orange zinnias make quite the pair with blue pimpernels.

✳ Green and red varieties of coleus create a season-long display of pretty foliage.

PRIMARY, SECONDARY, AND BEYOND!

✳ Primary: if you love playing with Crayola colors, try red celosia, yellow marigolds, and blue lobelia.

✳ Secondary: purple and orange pansies with green creeping Jenny spilling over the side of the pot looks fabulous at Halloween time.

✳ Tertiary: amber-colored coreopsis, false indigo, and the violet-red tassels of love-lies-bleeding would make a stunning combination for a large pot.

Picking the Right Pots

Besides the plants, the other main ingredients in any container combination are potting soil and pot. While potting soil doesn't have much influence on design, don't underestimate the pizzazz that the pot can bring to the combination. The pot will also be responsible for holding the only soil and water your plants have access to, so it's equally important to choose one that is the appropriate size, shape, and material.

When it comes to containers, the possibilities and permutations are endless.

Blue pots contrast nicely with orange calendula.

Black and white containers feel uptown and modern.

SIZE

If you're choosing a container for a plant that is still a seedling, you can use its original nursery pot as a guide. You want to select a container that is at least 4 inches wider and taller than the nursery pot, so that your plant has room to expand. But don't select a pot that is gigantic in comparison, as too much extra soil in the pot can cause it to become waterlogged and may lead to rotting roots. It's better to repot a plant in progressively larger pots as it grows.

Plants with vigorous root systems, such as trees and a few vegetables (tomatoes and broccoli come to mind), need pots that are at least 18 inches tall. The height of the pot is often more important for the aforementioned plants than the width of the pot, although an absurdly tall, narrow pot could be a problem too. If you're unsure of whether a plant needs extra room, go visit an independent garden center and talk to one of their knowledgeable employees. Many garden center employees have degrees in horticulture and loads of hands-on gardening experience—a great resource to keep in your back pocket (or at least on your speed dial).

The varying sizes of the metal containers add interest while still feeling unified.

This ponytail palm (*Beaucarnea recurvata*) is a perfect match for the round pot.

SHAPE

Squint your eyes when you're looking at a plant so that you can only see its most basic form. Is it a tall, skinny plant? A short, squat plant? A good general principle is to pair pots and plants that have a similar visual weight and shape: medium-sized plants with medium-sized pots, plants with a wide horizontal spread in wider pots, and so on. A small, rounded plant, for example, will probably look good in an equally squat pot (try saying that ten times fast!) but it would look silly in tall, narrow pot—like a scoop of ice cream on a cone. Contrasting pot and plant forms sometimes works too: that same squat pot might help a plant with a vertical habit look grounded. Just be careful that the pot is not radically out of proportion to its plant since this will often look unstable and may negatively affect the plant's health.

MATERIALS

The material of your container has a lot to do with personal aesthetic but it is also a major consideration in terms of helping plants thrive. Each material has its pros and cons, depending on the growing situation and plants.

FIBERGLASS AND RESIN offer the molded or carved look of ancient pottery without the inconvenience of lugging a heavy pot. These materials can also be more reasonably priced than their stone or clay counterparts.

METAL and modern are synonymous in the design world. You won't have to worry about containers cracking in the winter, but beware in the summer—metal pots can get very hot in full sun. Be sure to water your plants sufficiently or the roots will cook.

PLASTIC is the obvious choice for gardeners on a serious budget. It is also good if you live on the top floor of a building with no elevator, or have a weight restriction on your balcony. If you don't like the plastic look, consider painting the pot with a faux finish or stencil. However, if your balcony is very windy, small plastic pots may be easily blown over.

UNGLAZED TERRACOTTA is good for people who tend to overwater, as the clay wicks the excess water out of the soil quickly. It's also a smart choice for areas with extremely hot summers, as it can help shield roots from the heat. The downsides of terracotta are that it dries out quickly, can crack if left outside during winter, and tends to flake and crumble over time.

WOOD lends a specific feel to a garden, be it minimalist, natural, or rustic. Hardwoods are sturdy and will last, just don't let the container sit directly on the ground or in standing water since that will cause the wood to rot.

DESIGN CONSIDERATIONS

Do you want all your pots to match? An assortment of terracotta pots in different shapes, sizes, and textures (some have quilted patterns or scalloped edges) would feel classy without being stuffy or boring. You could do the same thing with other colors. All white or black pots looks more modern, while a collection of royal blue glazed pots lends a Mediterranean vibe.

If you're going to mix up your colors, do it carefully or go totally crazy—don't go halfway. I loved the combination of brightly colored glazed pots that I saw in Mexico: blue, yellow, orange, and red. You could select one or two centerpiece containers with vibrant patterns, and then choose solid-color pots for the rest of your plants. For a more sedate look, try narrowing the pot palette to just two colors, picking neutral colors, or choosing pots that are gradations of the same color.

You'll also want to consider which pot-to-plant color scheme will best suit your garden: monochromatic (pots that are the same color as the foliage or flowers) or contrasting (pots that stand apart, colorwise, from the plants). Monochromatic schemes are usually more serene and contemporary, while contrasting pots and plants are peppier and lend themselves to ethnic or tropical gardens.

Simple terracotta containers can bring a lot of design super power to your garden.

CHEAP POT UPGRADE 101

All you need is a little elbow grease,
a few craft supplies, and
some DIY spirit to transform three
plain-Jane pots into a cohesive container
collection that's as interesting
to look at as the plants themselves.
Choose from chalkboard, stencil,
or batik techniques.

Clockwise from bottom right:
the chalkboard, stencil, and
batik techniques.

CHALKBOARD

SUPPLIES

Terracotta pot

Smooth paint roller

Outdoor paint

Masking tape

Foam stamp

Chalkboard paint

METHOD

1. Using the paint roller, paint the area below the lip of the pot with the outdoor paint. Allow to dry completely.

2. Mark off a rectangle with masking tape and, with a clean paint roller, paint the area inside the rectangle with the chalkboard paint. Remove tape.

3. Using the paint roller, cover the foam stamp in an even coat of chalkboard paint and press it firmly into place. Repeat to complete your design. Allow the paint to dry overnight before planting.

STENCIL

SUPPLIES

Plastic pot

Spray paint

Pencil

Stencil

Stencil glue

Smooth paint roller

Outdoor paint

METHOD

1. Use the spray paint to apply the background color onto the pot in short, even strokes. Allow to dry completely.

2. Mark the placement of the stencil around the pot with light pencil marks.

3. Apply the stencil glue according to package instructions. Place the stencil in the first spot and smooth it down. Use the paint roller to apply an even coat of the outdoor paint all over the stencil. Skip a spot (so the stencil won't smudge wet paint) and repeat all the way around the pot. Allow the paint to dry overnight before planting.

BATIK

SUPPLIES

Terracotta pot

Smooth paint roller

Acrylic paint

Pencil

White puffy paint

Clear varnish

METHOD

1. Paint the entire pot with the acrylic paint. Allow to dry completely.

2. Sketch out a complex batik pattern in very light pencil marks; cover the entire area that you want to have the design.

3. Trace the penciled pattern with puffy paint. Allow to dry completely.

4. Apply clear varnish to the exterior of the entire pot. Allow to dry overnight before planting.

The stencil technique is equally striking on a larger planter box. Here, white bacopa and pink calibrachoa soften the edge of this upgraded planter.

Thinking Outside the Pot

Sometimes finding extra money for containers can be a bit like trying to squeeze blood out of a rock. But by letting your creative and resourceful juices flow, you'll find plenty of homes for your plants that aren't crazy expensive. In fact, if you repurpose ordinary household items, abandoned children's toys, or recycling bin inhabitants, the container might even be free. Remember to drill drainage holes in the bottom of your container if they don't already exist.

The inherent drainage of flour sifters (top) and colanders (bottom) makes for perfect succulent containers.

A plant-filled vintage birdcage blends seamlessly into the patio garden.

BIRDBATHS look really awesome planted with succulents or other rock garden plants like California poppies, sweet alyssum, and forget-me-nots. I've seen used ones listed in the classifieds for less than twenty dollars. Avian aficionados could also add garden character with a vintage birdcage: just lock in a potted plant instead of a feathery friend

COLANDERS AND FLOUR SIFTERS are just dying to become containers; after all, these kitchen stalwarts already have built-in drainage. Seek out vintage colanders in interesting colors—or spray paint one to suit your color scheme. Flour sifters planted with succulents or small herbs like thyme are truly charming.

LARGE SALAD BOWLS from the homewares section of your favorite department store are often a much more economical purchase than virtually identical pots. Just drill a hole in the bottom and treat yourself to some special plants with all that money you saved.

PORTABLE BARBEQUES designed for on-the-go adventures like camping trips or long days at the beach can be kept stationary and planted with herbs or succulents. See page 88 for project instructions.

RED WAGONS, like the one your kids haven't used in years, are fun, moveable containers—especially for succulents, whose shallow roots don't mind the lack of growing space. Use a hammer and nail or awl to punch drainage holes every six inches and pot that bad boy up. I've also seen a rusty old wheelbarrow planted with edibles; same idea and it looked fantastic!

SODA CANS were not part of my potting repertoire until I attended a class on frugal gardening during which the presenter described a street vendor in Mexico growing the succulent "string of pearls" in soda and beer cans. Coffee tins provide a bigger pot. The trick to achieving this cool, retro look is finding interesting cans or painting them a bright color.

TRASH CANS that are about half the size of the curbside kind will add an urban or industrial aesthetic to any space. Peruse local hardware store aisles for these galvanized goods and give your dwarf tree a first-rate home.

WINE BOXES make delightful containers for low-growing flowers, or shallow-rooted edibles like lettuces. If you buy wine in bulk—or have a friend at a wine shop—you'll have easy access to these wooden display boxes. Save your corks and use them as topdressing to reinforce the theme.

Basic Plant Composition

One-plant pots are pretty straightforward but it can get a little trickier to pick out multiple plants and combine them so that the pot looks amazing. Understanding composition is the art of understanding what people find to be visually appealing. It may sound scary and serious, but it's actually very empowering to have a strategy. A good starting point is to make sure your plant palette includes contrasting shapes, sizes, and textures. A planter filled with foliage and flowers that are too similar means you won't be able to fully appreciate the unique qualities of each plant. Instead, contrast one plant's large, broad leaves with another's small, finely cut foliage; complement large flowers with repeating sprays of diminutive blooms; or play heart-shaped leaves off spiky, strappy foliage. It's also important to make sure all the plants to be combined in one pot have similar light and water needs.

An easy way to create a balanced plant composition is to use the "thriller, filler, spiller" formula invented by former *Fine Gardening* editor Steve Silk. As you might suspect from the name, thrillers are leading ladies: tall, upright plants with some characteristic that makes your mouth water, like stunning flowers or jaw-dropping foliage color. Fillers, often billowy and finely textured, add lushness and provide a backdrop for thrillers to strut their stuff. The spiller's job is to flow over the sides, softening the edge of the pot and integrating plants with pot.

Pick plants with different shapes, textures, and colors of foliage to create visual interest.

A dazzling thriller (*Alocasia*), filler (*Strobilanthes dyerianus*), spiller (*Heliotrope*) composition.

Once you've picked plants that complement each other, you can play around with different methods of combining them in the pot. An easy technique is to center the thriller in the pot, and then surround it completely with spillers and fillers. For a modern or edgy container, try placing the thriller off to one side, the fillers next to it, and then any spillers flowing over the opposite side of the pot. Yet another approach is to balance the whole composition: situate the thriller in the center back, plant the fillers directly in front of it, and then put one spiller on either side of the pot. A comprehensive list of container-worthy thrillers, fillers, and spillers could fill this entire book, but here are a few of my top picks to get you started.

THRILLERS

✳ Canna (*Canna*). For thriller status, choose cannas with unusual flower colors, striped leaves, or striking foliage like that of deep burgundy-colored 'Black Knight'. Cannas will grow to approximately 5 feet tall if given a large enough pot. Container-hardy in zones 8 to 11, but tubers can be dug up and saved for next year.

✳ Elephant's ear (*Colocasia*). It's hard to find something more dramatic than these heart-shaped leaves as big (or bigger) than dinner plates. Elephant's ear will grow to 5 feet tall in a large container. Like cannas, the tubers can be dug up and stored for the winter. Container-hardy in zones 8 to 11.

✳ New Zealand flax (*Phormium*). Those with rigid upright leaves in striking bronze or variegated colors are definite showstoppers. Dwarf varieties grow to 24 inches tall and wide. Hardy in zones 7 to 11.

FILLERS

✳ Coleus (*Solenostemon*). Some varieties of coleus could really be thrillers, but I prefer using them as fillers in shady pots. Leaves come in colors like orange, green, magenta, and deep maroon, and plants range in size from 12 to 36 inches. Hardy in zones 10 and 11; treat as an annual elsewhere.

✳ Dill (*Anethum graveolens*). Feathery, finely cut leaves make a nice contribution to edible containers without demanding too much attention. If given a larger pot, dill can grow to 36 inches tall. Annual.

✳ Wormwood (*Artemisia absinthium*). I think of silver wormwood as the classy and sophisticated cousin of love-able dusty miller (Senecio cineraria). Wormwood forms 24- to 36-inch mounds and is container-hardy in zones 5 to 8.

SPILLERS

✳ Creeping Jenny (*Lysimachia nummularia*). My favorite small-leaved green spiller has pretty cascades of lime green, quarter-sized leaves. Forms low, dense mats that can cover 12 to 24 inches. Container-hardy in zones 4 to 8.

✳ Deadnettle (*Lamium*). Lime or white variegated leaves add a nice punch to shady gardens. The small pink or purple flowers are an added bonus. Airy, cascading mounds can reach 24 inches. Container-hardy in zones 4 to 8.

✳ Sweet potato vine (*Ipomoea batatas*). Maple-like or heart-shaped leaves in lime green or chocolately purple will trail over the side of the pot for up to 4 feet. Hardy in zones 9 to 11 in containers; treat as an annual in colder climates, or dig up the tubers and store them for the following year.

Anti-Boring Flooring

Apartment and condo dwellers creating gardens on balconies or small patios often think they're stuck with existing splintery wood or drab concrete flooring thanks to stringent renter or homeowners association rules. Even if your container garden is on your own home's front porch, it may not be financially or structurally possible to replace the flooring. Fortunately, numerous relatively inexpensive and impermanent options exist that will help you spruce up and add interest to your container garden's floor—all without causing trouble with landlords or HOA boards.

A rug designed for outdoor conditions is a good place to start. Your mind probably goes immediately toward sisal and other typical doormat materials, but don't stop there. I've seen zebra print outdoor fabric with a rubberized backing that would definitely add some excitement beneath your feet. Craftier gardeners could also buy a solid-colored outdoor rug and stencil or hand paint a pattern that coordinates with the space. Be sure to seal painted rugs with a clear varnish so your handiwork is protected.

An upscale, yet surprisingly affordable, flooring option is prefabricated wooden slats that are formed into 12-inch deck tiles. A special backing allows the tiles to simply snap together. You can cover an entire balcony or patio with the tiles for less than a few hundred dollars. And if you move or change your style, the tiles are as easy to remove as they were to install in the first place. Try searching for vendors online using the keywords: interlocking wooden deck tiles.

Paving a small courtyard with gravel—an economical and environmentally friendly material—is a familiar garden floor upgrade that could translate well to small, enclosed patios as well. Hardworking DIYers can transform a muddy pit into a usable space with interlocking paving stones. Loads of other unique flooring solutions are out there, often inspired by interior design websites and other unlikely sources. (If a kitchen floor can go from dingy to vintage with a painted black-and-white checkerboard pattern, why can't a balcony or porch?). And lastly, think from the floor up and consider a brightly painted accent wall as a way to enhance your space.

These attractive wooden deck tiles are a snap to put together.

The graphic black-and-white checkerboard pattern is an out-door flooring game changer.

You Have to Sit Somewhere!

What's the point of a beautiful outdoor garden if you don't have anywhere to sit down and enjoy it? I don't think it's possible to overstate the importance of providing a place to relax with a bagel, a cup of coffee, and a view of the gorgeous garden you've created.

Look for tables and chairs scaled for small spaces so you don't waste precious garden real estate with more furniture than you really need—sets marked "bistro" will be about the size of those at your favorite outdoor café. Another space-saving solution is to use chairs that can be folded up and stowed away when you don't need them. So if you live alone, leave just one chair out in the garden, but store another two or three in an indoor closet and just whip them out when friends come over. You can also buy tables that attach to the wall: flip the table out of the way when you're caring for your container garden, and flip it back up when you want to read a book or enjoy a glass of wine al fresco.

Choosing tables or seats that do double duty as storage is another way to get more from your space. There are attractive benches with removable lids so you can store tools or extra potting soil out of sight. Look for other opportunities to get two uses out of one piece of furniture, such as an arbor that provides shade and a trellis for plants, but also has a built-in bench for seating.

Matching sets of table and chairs help the space (especially if it's particularly small) look less cluttered. Your table and chairs are part of the overall design, so pick something that complements your plants and especially your containers. If you find great outdoor furniture that clashes with your color scheme (or say, chairs that don't match one another), keep in mind that spray paint is an easy remedy. Don't forget that comfort is important too. If need be, add colorful cushions to soften chairs or benches.

Smaller table and chair sets can add both a place to sit and a fun punch of color.

GARDEN UNDER GLASS

Speaking of furniture serving two purposes, why not coax a container into doing double duty? This simple project uses hardware store materials to turn an already planted container into a handy side table. Although perhaps not quite as luxurious as observing tropical fish through a boat's glass bottom, it's still nice to put your plants on display in such a useful manner. Because the sun's ultraviolet rays can scorch plants when magnified by glass, a table like this is best in bright shade.

SUPPLIES

Container planted with low-growing plants, such as succulents

6 (12-inch) pieces copper pipe

Round plexiglass tabletop (4 inches larger in diameter than container)

Builder's level

METHOD

1. Place the copper pipe pieces in evenly spaced intervals around the interior edge of the pot.

2. Push the pipe pieces securely into the soil so that they are sticking out approximately 8 inches above the pot.

3. Place the plexiglass tabletop on top of the pipe pieces, use a builder's level to check that the plexiglass is being held evenly above the pot.

Fun Garden Ornaments

Adding little jewels to stop and admire will make your garden more interesting.

Ornaments are to a garden what family photos and treasured tchotchkes are to a living room: the small things that make a space warm, give visitors a sense of your personality, and rekindle fond memories. In a small garden, the scale of your chosen ornaments is an important consideration. A large gazing ball might be perfectly fabulous tucked between plants out in the yard, but in an undersized container garden it would be awkwardly out of proportion. But that doesn't mean you should give up on gazing balls—just find a smaller one to nestle into a pot. This size-appropriate concept goes for any garden art you want to display, whether a Buddha statue or a garden gnome. You can add some height to your garden with small pieces of art on long stakes designed to be stuck into the soil. Whimsical bees, butterflies, birds, and dragonflies—or perhaps a laser-cut metal rose if your tastes are more modern—would be lovely towering over a flower pot.

It's also fun to look for opportunities to continue a collection you normally display indoors (or one that generally just gathers dust in a shoebox under your bed) out into your container garden. If you collect frogs, look for versions that are safe to keep outdoors and hide a few around your garden, to be discovered by visitors. I like creating little vignettes between my planters with the strange rocks that my husband has been bringing home from our vacations ever since he took a geology class in college. The rocks are beautiful in their own right, and they bring back memories of the great times we've spent together.

DRESS IT UP

Another way to include a bit of garden art in your small space is by finding artfully created utilitarian objects. A trellis could be a boring grid or it could show off some gorgeous woodworking or iron—why not use a rusty old gate? Or tie some branches together to make your own. Your trellis could even be a beautiful piece of art that just happens to host a scrambling vine. Same thing with plant markers: plastic tabs get the job done, but customized vintage silver cutlery would be a much more creative way to differentiate the 'Japanese Black Trifele' and 'Purple Cherokee' tomatoes.

If you crown your soil with a decorative topdressing instead of plain old mulch you'll still get most of the mulching benefits (soil moisture retention and reduced erosion) but with an unmistakable design kick. Topdressing ideas include sand, gravel, seashells, buttons, and marbles. Be creative— just don't use anything that could become toxic as it breaks down, especially when growing edibles.

A topdressing of colorful glass highlights the haworthia's unusually pale coloring.

Lighting Options

A charming lantern looks great during daylight hours too.

Outdoor lighting will help you get the most bang for your container garden buck. Early birds and night owls alike will appreciate being able to enjoy the garden at any time of the day. Lighting also adds a wonderful ambience to a space, and it draws your eye to focal points, such as a much loved plant or wonderful piece of garden art.

Since most balconies, patios, and porches don't have a power source (and even if they did, who wants wires going all over the place?), it's best to use solar-powered lights. Solar lighting comes in every conceivable design style, including hand-blown colored-glass globes that can double as garden art. Tuck small stake lights into pots to light a pathway or highlight a focal point, or place solar-powered table lights on top of garden furniture to provide dining ambiance. Don't forget to think up too: twist strings of solar-powered lights around tree trunks, across a balcony railing, or along the roof of the porch.

In addition to the latest solar technology, candles and tiki-style torches are terrific old-school options. Candlelight is very flattering and romantic, from the simple flicker of tall dripping candles to the intricately patterned glow escaping a wrought-iron Moroccan lantern. You probably want to avoid scented candles, lest they overpower the natural fragrance of your plants, but a citronella candle will help ward off mosquitoes. Torches that burn lamp or citronella oil come in a wide variety of styles, from traditional tiki to modern hand-blown glass torches. Simply stick the stakes into your pots in strategic locations and light the wicks whenever you want some added light. Always be careful that flammable items—especially your precious plants—are well out of the way of flames.

This balcony in British Columbia, Canada, is illuminated from the ground up.

Less SMALL, More SASSY

It's not news that most apartment and condo gardeners face the challenge of lack of space. After all, there is no such thing as a half-acre balcony, and even the most luxurious Manhattan rooftop terrace is nothing compared to a suburban lot. But don't accept the basic footprint of your balcony or patio as the final word on gardening space. You can double your square footage by borrowing air space that no one was using, or by employing other creative problem-solving tactics.

Magically expand the surfaces you have by using pots that straddle or otherwise attach themselves to railings and posts. The Greenbo is one of my favorite pots in this category—I love the bright colors it comes in and the modern styling. Window box planters that have a groove down the center are meant to be attached to the top of balcony and porch railings. You can also get inexpensive clips that screw into walls or wooden posts and then support regular terracotta pots. Heck, I once saw a bunch of large tin cans screwed into the wall and planted with geraniums. And you know what? It looked awesome!

Attaching a trellis to your wall is another way to take advantage of unoccupied vertical space. The trellis itself can be a beautiful addition to your container garden. Or use the built-in trellises that balcony and porch railings provide. Though, if you plan on moving in the near future, don't train a deeply loved plant along your balcony railing since you won't be taking it with you. Also keep in mind that landlords and homeowners associations tend to get cranky about things like growing plants on railings and attaching pots and planters to walls. I say it's easier to ask for forgiveness than for permission, but if you're more rule-abiding than I am, research restrictions before getting to work.

Greenbo planters beautify a balcony railing in Tel Aviv, Israel.

Like trellises, étagères and baker's racks add architectural interest while saving space. Look for them at garage sales or thrift shops, or buy new if you've got the cash to burn. Load the shelves with small pots and let vines interweave among the plants and onto the rack itself. In a similar vein, arbors are wonderful structures for training vines; simply flank the arbor with two large pots planted with vines such as passionflower (*Passiflora* spp.), sweetpea (*Lathyrus odoratus*), or even edible peas (*Pisum sativum*) and beans (*Phaseolus vulgaris*). If your arbor is sturdy enough, attach a hanging basket to enhance the sense of lushness. Underneath the ornamental arch is a great place for a small bench or chair where you can enjoy the shade created by the dense covering of plants. Depending on the type of space, an arbor could also define the entrance to your container garden, or frame a particularly beautiful view.

Window boxes hooked over a balcony railing add growing space to your garden.

THE ELEMENTS

Working with Weather and Climate

2

THE ELEMENTS—SUN, WIND, RAIN, FREEZING TEMPERATURES— are often harder on container gardens than they are on traditional gardens, but with a little planning you can overcome everything nature throws at you. Choosing plants that are well suited to your climate as well as the specific conditions on your balcony or patio is an important step toward insuring that your garden is over-the-top awesome.

I'd like to share a little parable about a fictional-but-all-too-common character: the eager gardener. It all starts when the eager gardener moves into a new apartment and giddily runs out to the balcony. Just looking around inspires rapid-fire images of gorgeous outdoor spaces but, overtaken by enthusiasm, our new gardener doesn't write any of these ideas down; no measurements or photos are taken either. Right after moving in, he or she flies across the country and while there picks up a regional magazine with lots of beautiful plants. Upon returning home, our gardener whips out Google and finds mail-order nurseries selling all of those stunning plants that are completely inappropriate for the eager gardener's climate.

Our eager gardener descends upon a local pottery discount center and buys a dozen pots, picking whichever strikes his or her fancy. No thought is given to size, weight, material, or how the pots work together and with the plants that were ordered. Whew. That was a whirlwind of buying, but now all the plants have arrived, the heavy pots were lugged up all three flights of stairs, and it's time to plant. The eager gardener quickly realizes that more plants have arrived than will fit on the balcony. No worries: half are given to friends and neighbors. It's also a bummer that the pots look mismatched, but it is still rewarding to care for the plants and spend time outside. That is, until winter comes. To our eager gardener's dismay, the plants are turning to brown mush after the first frost. Who knew that tropical plants like bananas can't survive a New England winter? Darn. I could go on with this balcony garden horror story, but I think you get the point. It's worth your time and money to plan ahead; you'll be happier with the results.

The Many Shades of Sun

Have you ever heard the myth that Eskimos have many different names for snow because it's such an important part of their lives? Well, gardeners are like that with sunshine. Direct light is unobstructed light shining—directly—onto the plant's leaves. Sunlight filtering through tree branches is known in the gardening world as "filtered light" or "dappled shade." And if your space receives light reflecting off a nearby building you probably have "bright shade."

Get your garden started on the right foot by picking plants suited to the amount of sunlight on your balcony or patio. The light needs of plants vary greatly: some are addicted to sunshine and need at least six hours, others are more shy and don't want a single minute of sunlight, and the rest want something in between. While many gardening hurdles can be conquered, it's nearly impossible to get full-sun plants to thrive on a full-shade balcony—or to prevent full-shade plants from roasting on a full-sun patio.

SUN MAPPING

Before heading out to the garden center, figure out how much sun your space gets. It's quite helpful to create a rough sketch of your garden and simply stick your head out every hour or two and take note of which parts are sunny or shaded throughout the day. As you garden in that space over the coming months, add notes about how the sun changes throughout the year. You are likely to find that some parts of the garden are much sunnier than others, that some areas are sunnier during different times of the day, and that the amount of sun your garden gets in fall and winter isn't the same as spring and summer. Don't forget that light reflects off shiny surfaces and light-colored walls, and may make things brighter.

If you're not around during much of the day to look for yourself, a variety of gadgets (such as the "Sunlight Calculator" or the "SunStick") can help you identify how much sun your space typically gets. Basically, these gadgets are equipped with a sensor that reads how much sunlight the area in which it is placed receives. Then, at the end of the day, the gadget indicates what type of plants will grow there. Place this gadget in several different spots and make notes on your sun-map sketch of which parts of the garden get sun and which are more shaded.

For the quickest, most low-tech approach, simply make an educated guess based on the direction your balcony or patio faces. Unobstructed south- and west-facing gardens usually get at least 6 hours of sun; choose full-sun and some tough part-sun plants. East-facing gardens only get morning sun, so pick full-sun or part-sun plants that can't handle afternoon heat. North-facing gardens are usually the shadiest; choose part-shade and full-shade plants.

PLANT TAG LINGO

Be sure to take a careful look at plant tags and only buy the plants that want the same amount of sunlight that your garden has to offer. Your sun-map sketch will really help you at this stage of the game. If you know what percentage of your garden space gets full sun versus part or full shade, you'll be able to make better plant-buying decisions.

FULL SUN: plants need more than 6 hours of direct sunlight. Sometimes plants that like full sun in a mild climate will do better in partial shade in a hotter climate.

PARTIAL SUN OR PARTIAL SHADE: plants need 3 to 6 hours of sun; the terms are often used interchangeably. If your space gets a continuous stream of light filtered through the branches of a tree or a similar obstruction, choose plants that need part sun or part shade.

FULL SHADE: plants can usually tolerate a small amount of indirect light filtered through tree branches or trellises.

Placing sensitive plants underneath a table or bench, or next to a taller plant, helps provide shade during the hottest part of the day.

MIRIAM'S *morning* SUN DECK

Miriam Settles and her husband live in an Alexandria, Virginia, townhouse. On their second-story deck she grows all sorts of plants, from Japanese maples, hydrangeas, and butterfly bushes to herbs, tomatillos, and strawberries. Miriam's love of gardening was sparked in the early 1990s when she was living in a little house on an Air Force base in Dayton, Ohio. While Miriam's mom was visiting, she took pity on her bare garden beds and dragged her to the garden center to pick out a few plants and seeds. Since then, Miriam has gardened everywhere she and her husband have lived, no matter how small the space—even when it was just a minuscule deck with window boxes covering every inch of the railing.

Now Miriam is lucky to have a 12-by-20 foot deck that faces east and gets six hours of morning sun. Miriam feels that getting morning sun is ideal for container gardening because she still gets a full six hours of sunshine, but her plants are protected from scorching afternoon heat. In the summer, Miriam's deck is transformed into a mini oasis. She spends as much time as possible among her beautiful plants, even eating meals outdoors at her small table.

Winters in Alexandria aren't usually too cold, but occasionally Miriam faces the challenge of a frigid winter. She has decided not to go to any extra effort to keep her plants alive over the winter. If they survive, they survive. If they die, they die. Because she doesn't give her containers added winter protection, Miriam chooses perennials that are hardy to zone 5 even though she lives in zone 7. The two-zone buffer gives her plants a better shot at making it.

Miriam sometimes plants up to twelve plants in one pot; she also likes to mix perennial flowers with herbs. The results are gorgeous!

Climate Survival Skills

Good garden centers will sell only those plants that do well in the surrounding area. But what if you want to order seeds or plants from a catalog or website? The best way to find out which plants will grow in your neck of the woods is to determine which zone you are gardening in and choose plants meant for your zone.

The United States Department of Agriculture (USDA) has devised a system of growing zones based on lowest winter temperatures. Right off the bat you can probably see the major flaw in the USDA zone system: it is only concerned with lowest winter temperatures. Obviously some places have similar winters but different springs, summers, and falls. And not all cold days are created equal: a 20 degree F day with plentiful sunshine feels a lot different than the same temperature with a foot of snow on the ground and strong gusts of wind. Use the USDA zones as a starting point, not the final word on what will thrive where you live.

If you can't pinpoint your exact location on the USDA hardiness zone map, I suggest checking out a website like garden.org/zipzone, which uses your zip code to determine your zone. Once you have the zone number, it will help figure out whether a plant is well suited to your particular area. You might have seen a plant tag that says something like "hardy to zone 5." This means that the plant can generally be expected to live through zone 5 winters, and the winters of all higher-numbered zones (but not the winters of lower-numbered zones).

Some plants actually need a cold winter, and the USDA zone system can also be used to provide that information. For example, you might see a plant tag that says, "suitable for zones 5 to 7." This means that the plant in question really needs the winter temperatures found in those zones. If you live in zone 8 and you buy a plant that says "zones 5 to 7" the plant will probably not produce as many flowers or fruit as it would in the right zone. And may not produce any at all.

A zonal range can also mean that the plant in question does not do well in zones with a warmer summer than the higher number in the range. However, the USDA did not consider summer temperatures at all when creating its zone system, so don't be discouraged if you are only one zone away from the plant's ideal range. If you discover such a plant, it's worth trying it out in a cooler part of your balcony. Many times, a plant that generally likes summers cooler than those in your area can be made happy by putting it in a spot with morning sun and afternoon shade.

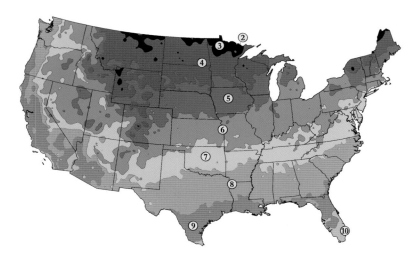

The United States Department of Agriculture has assigned the entire country a zone based on the average winter temperature of each area. Similar maps can be found for other countries.

The Big Chill

Here's another twist on USDA zones that only applies to container gardeners. A plant tag that describes a plant's cold hardiness is talking about plants growing in the ground—soil is almost always warmer than the air just above it. That means that container-grown plants are actually living in a climate that is slightly colder than that of the plants growing in the ground just a few feet away. To deal with the discrepancy between ground and air temperature it's helpful to avoid plants that are barely hardy in your zone. So, if you live in zone 6, steer clear of plants that are only hardy to zone 6 and stick with plants that are hardy to at least zone 5. Try to keep a one- to two-zone buffer. Being conservative when it comes to zone hardiness will reduce the number of plants that die on your watch.

You may also want to wrap your pots in insulation during the winter. Regular bubble wrap works just fine, or you can purchase special foil-lined horticultural bubble wrap from garden centers. Simply wrap the container with bubble wrap and tie it in place. When possible, bring the bubble wrap over the top of the container, and secure it around the base of the plants. This will help protect the pot from the freezing-and-thawing cycle that usually happens at the end of winter. Get your bubble wrap on after the pot freezes if the plants are hardy, if the plants in your container are half-hardy, be sure to wrap them up before they freeze.

Another option is to bring moveable plants indoors for the winter. Many hardy plants go dormant in the winter and can safely be stored in a garage or other unheated, poorly lit storage areas. Others can be overwintered near your brightest windows. If you have pets or small children, be sure that you're not bringing any poisonous plants inside. And of course, there's the simplest and most extravagant solution: treat the plants that aren't really meant for your zone as annuals and expect them to die at the end of the season. If they make it to next spring, act pleasantly surprised.

COLD-CLIMATE CONTAINER FARMING

In colder locations with short summers (for example, Minneapolis, Minnesota, or Portland, Maine) it can be a challenge to find fruits and vegetables that will produce their bounty fast enough to be harvestable before cold autumn temperatures halt the plant's growth. But don't let that stop

Many plants that are not able to withstand freezing temperatures will happily overwinter inside, next to a bright window.

you from growing your own food. Instead, employ a multi-pronged approach: choose plants that naturally mature quickly, select varieties of heat-loving plants that mature in less than 90 days, and either start seeds indoors earlier in the season or buy transplants.

Naturally fast-growing edibles include carrots (many varieties only need 60 days), radishes (20 to 30 days to maturity), and salad greens (20 to 50 days to maturity). Basil, oregano, and many other herbs are fast growers too. The cultivar names of traditionally heat-loving plants (such as tomatoes, peppers, and eggplant) that have been bred to mature quickly or to tolerate cooler summers often contain keywords (arctic, mountain, north) alluding to cold weather. The word "early" might also appear in the plant's name, like 'Early Cascade' tomato and 'Park's Early Thickset' bell pepper which mature at 55 and 60 days, respectively.

A potted lavender plant braves the elements.

If you live somewhere with short summers, choose fast-maturing varieties of heat-loving plants, such as peppers.

Other Climate Scenarios

Coleus is a real rock star when it comes to thriving in humid environments.

Humidity and very dry air are another two things that the USDA zone system doesn't take into consideration. Most of the ultra-humid southern United States, for example, falls into zone 8 or 9, while much of southern Arizona (land of super dry heat) shares the same two zones.

HUMIDITY

Mold, fungi, and bacteria thrive in warm, moist environments, which is a real bummer for container gardeners who live in humid climates. To avoid problems from the get go, look for plants that come from humid tropical and subtropical areas, or those described as mildew resistant, such as 'Green Ice' miniature rose. It's also wise not to mulch or topdress right up to the base of your plants—this tends to become a four-star hotel for bacteria, fungi, and mold.

Another consideration for choosing plants that do well with lots of humidity is whether the plant likes consistently moist soil, or wants to dry out between watering. Many succulents and cacti like to have fairly dry soil most of the time. They don't like having "wet feet," and if your summers are hot, rainy, and humid, you'll be hard pressed to provide what they want. On the other hand, some plants complain loudly the second their potting soil is only a tiny bit dried out. These plants will be your best friends: philodendrons (my favorite is *Philodendron* 'Prince of Orange'), coleus (*Solenostemon* spp.), daylilies (*Hemerocallis* spp.), and compact varieties of hibiscus (*Hibiscus rosa-sinensis*).

DRY HEAT

On the flipside of the humidity problem are very dry climates, which often go hand in hand with scorching heat. Keeping plants properly watered and preventing the roots from frying are major challenges. One way to help solve both of these problems is to double bag your container plants. Simply choose a nice outer pot and fill it with an inch or two of wood chips. Then place a slightly smaller inexpensive plastic pot inside the outer pot, and grow your plants in the inner pot. Fill in the gap between the inner and outer pots with more wood chips and during the height of summer, keep the wood chips damp. The barrier of moist wood chips will help keep soil temperatures down in the inner pot. Mulch or topdressing will also help prevent rapid evaporation of water in the soil.

While succulents and cacti are not well suited to humid climates, they are madly in love with hot, arid climates. Other plants that do splendidly in containers and prefer a drier climate include California poppy (*Eschscholzia californica*), lamb's ear (*Stachys byzantina*), shasta daisy (*Leucanthemum* spp.), lavender (*Lavandula* spp.), and tickseed (*Coreopsis* spp.).

Tickseed (*Coreopsis* spp.) thrives in hot, dry climates.

A dense planting of ficus is an effective windbreak.

Wind

On windy, exposed rooftops, larger, heavier furniture and planter boxes are less likely to be knocked over.

In urban areas, wind is funneled in between and forced over buildings and can really rip through container gardens, especially on high-floor balconies and rooftops. Wind poses several potential problems: it can damage plants by ripping off leaves or breaking branches, it can tear off flowers before they can be pollinated (and no pollination means no fruit), it can be cold (problematic if you're trying to grow warm season vegetables or flowers), and it can dry out plants and soil.

Large, heavy pots are less likely to be blown over by strong gusts of wind, and for that reason they are an excellent choice for container gardeners in windy climates. If it's necessary to use lightweight pots because of weight restrictions (or if that's just what you happen to have and love), you can screw a small hook-and-eye bolt to balcony or porch railings, or to a wall, and wire the planter to the structure. This is also a great way to deter thieves if your plants are somewhere accessible to unscrupulous passersby.

Regardless of whether or not you live in a windy area, never put a pot on the edge of a balcony railing or on top of a wall where it could fall on other people. Freak gusts of wind can happen anytime—as can incidents of human clumsiness. Your plant is unlikely to survive such a fall, and the potential to hurt someone below isn't worth the risk. If you want to expand your gardening space, be sure to securely fix the pot onto the railing or wall so it can't fall off.

PROTECTING FROM WIND DAMAGE

Anything solid positioned between your garden and the direction of the wind helps stop plants from being whipped around. To block wind coming through balcony railings, purchase pieces of clear plexiglass, drill holes in the corners, and use zip ties to affix plexiglass to the railing. Likewise, bamboo mats would provide comparable protection with a more natural-looking aesthetic.

You can also use plants as windbreaks, like a planter box filled with a dense hedge of shrubbery or bamboo along the edge of a balcony. This will help reduce the wind flow in the area on the other side of the windbreak. You'll then be able to place items like small pots or lightweight garden furniture on your balcony with less risk of them being blown over.

To help protect young seedlings from wind you can arrange them in a sturdy tomato cage that has been wrapped on the outside with clear plastic. Poke a few small holes in the plastic to allow some air to get through. This air flow will help prevent diseases from taking hold and also strengthen the stems of the plant without breaking them.

Shredded bark is a common type of mulch.

KEEPING SOIL MOIST

The more the wind dries out the plant's leaves, the harder the plant will try and draw up more water from the soil. If a lot of wind blows through your container garden, it's important to take extra steps to keep your potting soil from drying out. A practical place to start is by selecting fiberglass, plastic, or glazed ceramic containers, all of which do a good job of retaining soil moisture levels. Unglazed ceramic and terra-cotta pots will exacerbate the problem: as the wind dries the exterior of the pot these materials continue to draw out more and more water until the soil is bone dry. Wind also dries out uncovered soil, compounding the problem. Adding a protective layer of mulch—like shredded bark or dried leaves—will help retain moisture near the roots of plants, as well as add nutrients back into the soil and keep weeds at bay.

A low-budget way to protect seedlings is to cover the surface of your pot with a piece of black plastic from a cut-up trash bag (use white plastic if you live in the desert). Fill the pot all the way to the rim with soil and mix in slow-release fertilizer. Secure the plastic over the soil with a large rubber band so that the plastic is taut. In the middle of the plastic, use a sharp knife to cut an X that is just large enough to dig a hole and plant the seedling.

Rain

Heavy rains can be particularly tough on balcony and patio gardens. I used to garden on a patio two stories below the overhang of my apartment building. During big storms, rain would pour from that overhang and blast my plants like a hose, ripping off leaves and washing every iota of soil out of smaller pots.

To minimize damage to your container garden, take action before big storms start by moving your pots indoors, completely under the overhang, or completely exposed to the sky (it's better for a pot to get the full brunt of a rain storm than to be partially underneath the overhang and get the full brunt of water running off the roof). The smallest pots often get hit by a double whammy—first beaten down by the rain, and then, if it is raining particularly hard, water splashing up from the concrete—so if possible, put the small pots in the driest spot.

When you know rain is coming, avoid watering your pots. If the soil is already moist, then it will easily become waterlogged with even a little rain. Also, pots that have gravel or heavier mulch covering their soil don't get as waterlogged and don't have their soil washed away as much as pots without any topdressing. Another helpful method is to raise pots slightly off the ground with pot feet; this is a good practice in general and will help water drain out of the pot more quickly after a rain storm.

You can protect tender seedlings that can't be moved with plastic sheeting, upturned plastic nursery pots, or even clean yogurt cups. Plastic sheeting is the best method if you're trying to cover a large number of seedlings. Stick short bamboo stakes in several places and drape the sheeting over the stakes. Then weigh down the edges of the sheeting with heavy items such as pots, rocks, or bricks.

Remnants of a light rain on a collection of salad greens.

As you can see, knowledge is power! Knowing your garden space, understanding your light exposure and climate, and having a plan to deal with weather-related challenges before they present themselves will lead to more container-garden success. The best thing you can do if you are still coloring up your green thumb is to shun discouragement when a plant passes to the other side. Try and figure out what exactly happened and how a different plant or a better weather plan might produce more satisfying results next time.

THE BIRDS AND THE BEES

Attracting Wildlife to Your Garden

3

The idiom "the birds and the bees" came to mean what it does because birds and bees are so visibly involved in the circle of life—fertilizing flowers, helping spread seeds, creating nests, laying eggs—but in urban areas, wildlife is sometimes more a figment of our collective imagination than a perceptible presence. Fortunately, by choosing the right plants and gardening in an environmentally friendly manner, you can give nature a helping hand without neglecting your desire for beauty. The thrill of seeing a hummingbird at your feeder, a bee practically drunk with nectar zigzagging between flowers, or a butterfly flitting from plant to plant is well worth the effort of attracting them to your container garden.

The National Wildlife Foundation has a certification program that guides homeowners in their efforts to create a wildlife-friendly yard. In a nutshell, a certified wildlife habitat is a place for the entire lifecycle of a species to occur, so the NWF requires that it include food sources for wildlife, a water supply, places for wildlife to hide and raise their young, and for it to be maintained with environmentally friendly practices. I see no reason we can't use the same guidelines as inspiration when creating our balcony, patio, porch, or rooftop terrace gardens. It's amazing how many beneficial insects, birds, reptiles, and small animals thrive in the middle of the city, and how quickly they will find your garden if you just do a few things to make them feel welcome.

If you grow it, they will come. Here: a gazania flower heavily laden with ladybugs.

Food for Flight

Butterflies enjoy stopping by chrysanthemums for a nectar drink.

It can often be a challenge to keep wildlife from eating your plants, so providing food sources is the easiest part of creating a wildlife sanctuary. The best way to attract birds, bees, and butterflies is to use native plants. The Lady Bird Johnson Wildflower Center and the NWF both have native plant finders on their websites (see Resources). Also be sure to select heirloom varieties and cottage garden favorites for your wildlife garden. Many modern sunflowers, for example, have been bred to have no pollen at all. What a disappointment that must be to the wildlife that stops by those plants. But the varieties of sunflowers your grandmother and her friends grew? Whoa Nelly! They have lots of pollen for bees, and later in the season, those heirloom sunflowers make seeds that birds absolutely adore.

THE BIRDS AND THE BEES

A tiger swallowtail butterfly visiting black-eyed Susan flowers.

A variegated fritillary on butterfly weed.

CONTAINER PLANTS FOR BUTTERFLIES

Butterflies are typically attracted to flowers that face upward, with the center of the flower (where the pollen and nectar are stored) exposed to the sky. These types of flowers are easy for them to land on and insert their mouthparts for a sip of nectar. Avoid flowers that are tubular in shape because butterflies can't crawl into the area where the nectar is, the way bees can, and they don't have the specialized beak that hummingbirds use to drink from those sorts of flowers.

Different butterflies like the nectar from different flowers. To get a diverse group of butterflies, select a variety of plants known to attract them. Try picking plants that bloom on a staggered schedule so that flowers will always be available for a butterfly drink. Also, groups of the same plant are more likely to be noticed by butterflies than just one butterfly-friendly plant.

Appleblossom grass

(*Gaura lindheimeri*).
Many butterflies—including duskywings, red-banded hair-streaks, and skippers—adore the glorious pink foam of flowers that appleblossom grass will produce. The plants are only about 15 inches tall, but the flower wands stretch up another 12 inches. Container-hardy in zones 7 to 9.

Black-eyed Susan

(*Rudbeckia hirta*).
Gorgeous gold flowers with brown centers will satiate both the gardener's desire for beauty and the butterfly's need for nectar. Perfect for containers are dwarf varieties like *Rudbeckia hirta* 'Viette's Little Suzy' which only gets to 18 inches tall. Hardy to zone 5 in containers.

Butterfly weed

(*Asclepias tuberosa*).
If you live in the path of the Monarch butterfly, plant a few pots of aptly named butterfly weed. The bright orange flat-topped flowers grow 24 inches tall in all but the deepest pots (where they can reach 36 inches). Hardy in zones 5 to 10 in containers.

Chrysanthemums

(*Chrysanthemum* spp.).
Available in a mind-boggling array of different forms, chrysanthemums are highly revered around the world—in the southern United States there are even parades to celebrate this plant. Luckily, many butterflies agree with the hype. Choose from several dwarf varieties under 15 inches tall, such as 'Molimba' marguerite daisy (*C. frutescens* 'Molimba'). Another chrysanthemum benefit is that they're just as edible to humans as butterflies: try adding the slightly bitter flowers to salads, or include them in a vegetarian fondue spread with an Asian-style dipping sauce. Unless you're lucky enough to live in zones 10 or 11, treat as an annual.

St. John's wort

(*Hypericum perforatum*).
Butterflies love the nectar that comes along with the showy tufts of yellow stamens. St. John's wort blooms for about 6 weeks, topping out at about 24 inches tall. Hardy in zones 5 to 8 when grown in containers.

THE BIRDS AND THE BEES

Wildlife lives in urban areas too.
Considering they were here first, it
would be nice to help support them
along their way.

Flower bud on 'Marmalade' heuchera.

Bees, moths, butterflies, and hummingbirds will visit your salvia plant on a regular basis.

CONTAINER PLANTS FOR BIRDS

Birds look for plants that provide seeds and berries to keep their bellies full. Your feathered guests will be especially happy if you give them something to snack on during winter by growing bushes, like holly, that produce edible (to them) berries that are left on the plant.

Asters (*Aster* spp.) provide flowers that you'll enjoy in late summer and fall, as well as seeds for songbirds and nesting material. While birds love them, you'll also see bees and butterflies stopping by too. I'm especially fond of the wonderfully scented aromatic aster (*A. oblongifolius*) that forms 2 foot mounds; hardy in zones 4 to 9 in containers.

Coral bells (*Heuchera* spp.). Long wands of white or pink flowers appear in spring and lure hummingbirds like crazy. Check out sexy 'Dolce Blackcurrant' with its frosted black leaves (container-hardy in zones 5 to 9), or the warm orange and rust tones of 'Marmalade' (container-hardy in zones 5 to 11). Both plants form low mounds under 12 inches.

Mexican honeysuckle (*Justicia spicigera*). An excellent hummingbird plant for hot, arid climates, Mexican honeysuckle can be found growing naturally as a 6 foot shrub (feel free to prune hard to keep it a size you can manage) or trained as a patio tree. Container-hardy in zones 9 to 11.

Ornamental sages (*Salvia* spp.). Two words: hummingbird magnet. Hummingbirds especially love the beautiful red flower spikes of pineapple sage (*S. elegans*), whose leaves smell exactly as you would expect (hardy in zones 9 to 11). I am particular to blue anise sage (*S. guaranitica* 'Black and Blue'), which produces gorgeous tubular flowers and is container-hardy in zones 8 to 11. Plants range from just 12 inches to over 36 inches tall. Though they respond very well to hard pruning.

Winterberry holly (*Ilex verticillata*). This plant produces red berries that hold well into winter (hence the common name) and are enjoyed by cedar waxwings, bluebirds, and robins. If you plant winterberry shrubs in several large planter boxes, they will grow quite tall and form a nice privacy screen. Container-hardy in zones 5 to 9.

MOD-MINIMALIST BIRD FEEDER

The simple, clean lines of this square bird feeder make a classy contrast to all the vibrant, wildlife-friendly plants. A paint job inspired by artist Piet Mondrian's black and primary color palette would add another level to the minimalist theme. Regardless of how pleasing the end results are to the human eye, remember that birds will only show their enthusiasm when the feeder is stocked with delectable seed.

SUPPLIES

4 (1-foot) lengths 1 x 2 wood

4 (1½-inch) galvanized screws

Linseed oil

Multi-surface heavy duty glue, such as Gorilla Glue

Small ceramic pot without a drainage hole

1 hook bolt

Birdseed

METHOD

1. Screw the 4 pieces of 1 x 2 wood together to make a square frame.

2. Seal the wood with linseed oil.

3. Run a bead of glue around the bottom inner edge of the ceramic pot. Place the pot in the center of the bottom of the frame and wiggle gently to make sure there is good contact between the glue, the pot, and the wood frame. Allow the glue to completely harden before proceeding.

4. Screw the hook bolt into the top of the frame, directly above the pot. Add birdseed to the ceramic pot and hang the feeder outside. Enjoy watching birds discover your feeder!

Bees have no issues with the tubular shape of cerinthe flowers.

Plant rosemary to bring on the bees and keep your trimmings for use in the kitchen.

CONTAINER PLANTS FOR BEES

Try to plant at least ten plants that bees like, as this seems to be my magic number for attracting bees. Also, if your bee garden blooms year round it will be better able to support bees when other sources of pollen and nectar become scarce. Supporting honey bees—a European import—is especially important as Colony Collapse Disorder has had a huge, negative impact on these important crop pollinators. You can also support native mason bees by planting fruit trees, roses, strawberries, and raspberries, as well as providing nesting boxes.

Lavender's wonderfully fragrant flowers attract lots of bees and other beneficial insects.

Borage (*Borago officinalis*) is so beloved by bees that it's sometimes referred to as bee's bread. Plant a few pots and you're sure to see bees hovering around the blue flowers loaded with nectar. This easy-to-grow annual can reach 18 inches tall.

Greek cerinthe (*Cerinthe retorta*). For the longest time, I thought this plant's speckled blue-green leaves were its best feature. That is, until it sent up dozens of arching flower spikes covered with intense blue flower bracts and diminutive, yellow, tube-shaped flowers. Greek cerinthe forms an airy 36-inch mound. It's an annual, but will drop its seed freely in the pot, and if you live in a mild climate, you can have a blooming cerinthe year round. *C. major* is an equally delightful relative.

Lavender (*Lavandula* spp.) always seems to bring romantic images to mind so it's never hard to convince gardeners to plant these aromatic, bee-adored beauties. Gloriously scented English lavenders (*L. angustifolia*) are the most compact type of lavender and also the hardiest (suitable for zones 5 to 11). *L. angustifolia* 'Munstead Dwarf' is especially happy in a pot and grows to just 12 inches tall. Spanish lavender (*L. stoechas*) and French lavender (*L. dentata*) can also be successfully grown in a container, just know that they may have to be repotted every few years. Spanish and French lavenders are both particularly suited to hot, dry climates and are container-hardy in zones 8 to 11.

Rosemary (*Rosmarinus officinalis*). Bees absolutely can't get enough of rosemary when it's in bloom. In some climates the plants can grow to 4 feet tall but almost no one lets them get that big in a small space. Rosemary is container-hardy in zones 8 to 10; it can be overwintered near a bright window.

Rue (*Ruta graveolens*). A plant long known to humans—even mentioned in Shakespeare's "Hamlet"—rue has been popular among bees even longer. Rue has charming blue-green foliage and yellow flowers which reach 18 to 24 inches tall. Container-hardy in zones 7 to 11.

Wallflower (*Erysimum cheiri*) may be the nickname for someone who won't mingle at a party, but bees are not at all bashful about enjoying the plant's delicious nectar and pollen. This charming English cottage garden plant grows to 24 inches tall and easily reseeds itself (free plants!). Container-hardy in zones 6 to 9.

Hiding Places and Water Sources

Providing true hiding places for wildlife is probably the most challenging tenet of the NWF guidelines to recreate in a small-space container garden, but there are ways to encourage wildlife to feel secure enough to taste your plants or take a drink from your birdbath. Shrubs, such as holly, which do double duty as both hiding spot and food source are great choices for small spaces. You can try putting an actual birdhouse somewhere in your garden; ultimate do-it-yourselfers can even grow gourds and hollow them into birdhouses. Supplying nesting boxes for solitary (non-aggressive) mason bees is an effective way to persuade these exceptional pollinators to stick around your garden.

Traditional gardeners might provide a water source for wildlife with a pond or rain garden, but the easiest and most realistic way for balcony or patio gardeners is to include a birdbath. More than just birds will use your birdbath. I've seen bees and butterflies stopping by mine for a sip. To invite birds into your bathing accommodations, don't crowd a lot of plants around the birdbath. Birds look at that brush and think: "predator hiding spot."

Another option for adding a water source to your balcony is to have a "pond in a pot." Select a pot without a drainage hole, fill it with water, and place water plants in the pot. You may need to submerge a brick into the pot and place some of your water plants on top of the brick to keep them at the right height. If you're having a hard time finding water plants, check out the aquarium section of your local pet store.

A nesting box for mason bees.

STYLISH
DIY BIRDBATH

This simple birdbath will fit in the smallest pocket of space. To make it easier for creatures to refresh themselves, be sure to place a flat object, like a river rock, in the water. A river rock can supply birds a place to land, or serve as a stepping stone out of the water for overeager insects.

SUPPLIES

Terracotta pot and saucer

Ceramic adhesive with built-in applicator

Semi-gloss outdoor paint

Sponge paint brush

METHOD

1. Apply a generous ring of ceramic adhesive to the bottom of the pot.

2. Turn the saucer upside down on your work surface and center the bottom of the pot on the center of the saucer. Wiggle the pot once it is in place to ensure that you have good contact between the adhesive, saucer, and pot. Let dry for several hours.

3. Apply two thin coats of paint to all exterior surfaces. Allow to dry completely, then add water and rocks to bath.

Wildlife Garden Care and Maintenance

The care needed for a wildlife garden is not the exact same as a typical container garden. In a garden designed purely for your enjoyment, you might want to snip off damaged leaves or flowers past their prime and encourage the plant to grow new healthy leaves and flowers. But if you snip off a leaf that has been munched on by a caterpillar in a wildlife-supporting container garden, you could be inadvertently throwing out the caterpillar too, as well as a leaf that could still be nibbled on by other creatures. Talk about throwing out the baby with the bathwater! Even if the damage is done by a true pest—an insect or animal that you didn't want to attract—try to leave it alone, it may very well be food for some other animal or

insect. For example, unbeknownst to you, a ladybug may have spotted an aphid infestation and laid all of her eggs nearby, so that they'll have a good food source when they hatch. Ladybugs are so much fun to see in the garden; it would be a shame to take away their dinner.

It's the same thing with spent flowers. Nature is a brilliantly designed system, and different animals utilize flowers at different stages of life. Bees, butterflies, and other nectar-drinking, pollen-eating insects use flowers when they are open and beautiful. But other animals are waiting for the flower to turn into a seedpod, berry, or fruit before they'll eat it. You may feel crushed that your beautiful flowers now look haggard and are being pecked at and pulled apart by hungry birds, but remember, the plant evolved to have its flowers eaten by animals so that they will spread the plant's seed. Leave your plants alone, and try to find enjoyment in watching nature's perfectly orchestrated cycle of life.

ENVIRONMENTALLY FRIENDLY PRACTICES

Finally, all will be for naught if you don't garden in an environmentally friendly way. With a commitment to letting insects and animals eat your plants and flowers, it is more important than ever to avoid using chemical pesticides on your plants. You wouldn't want a Monarch caterpillar to munch on a leaf that is coated in pesticides. If you can, resist even organic pest control options, like insecticidal soap. All parts of your container garden will be used by the wildlife you want to attract. Birds actually enjoy eating snails, why deny them the pleasure?

Likewise, it is extra important in a wildlife-friendly container garden to use organic and natural methods of fertilizing your plants. Most synthetic fertilizers are used in excess, and end up as phosphorus and nitrate pollution in nearby water sources and ground water. Even runoff from an urban balcony far away from a natural body of water can potentially reach a river, lake, or ocean by way of storm drains. It is futile to feed your plants in such a manner that will contaminate the surrounding environment.

A garden that all sorts of winged creatures will definitely keep their eyes on.

Birds and the Bees Patio

Watch birds, bees, and butterflies flit about the garden year round, or throw open the door and join them. The two benches—which do double duty providing storage underneath—are the perfect place to read a book or enjoy a glass of lemonade with a friend. If you're lucky, you'll soon be joined by birds eating from your feeder or splashing around in your birdbath. This design, brimming with a colorful palette of plants, will lure wildlife while pleasing your senses. Leave the berries and seedpods on the plants during winter to provide interest for you and food for the local birds.

COMMON NAME	SCIENTIFIC NAME	NUMBER OF PLANTS
Appleblossom grass	*Gaura lindheimeri*	6
Black-eyed Susan	*Rudbeckia hirta* 'Viette's Little Suzy'	3
Borage	*Borago officinalis*	3
Chrysanthemum	*Chrysanthemum frutescens* 'Molimba'	1
Lavender	*Lavandula angustifolia* 'Munstead Dwarf'	2
Mexican honeysuckle	*Justicia spicigera*	1
Pineapple sage	*Salvia elegans*	3
Rosemary	*Rosmarinus officinalis*	1
Rue	*Ruta graveolens*	1
Sweet alyssum	*Lobularia maritima*	3
Winterberry	*Ilex verticillata*	1

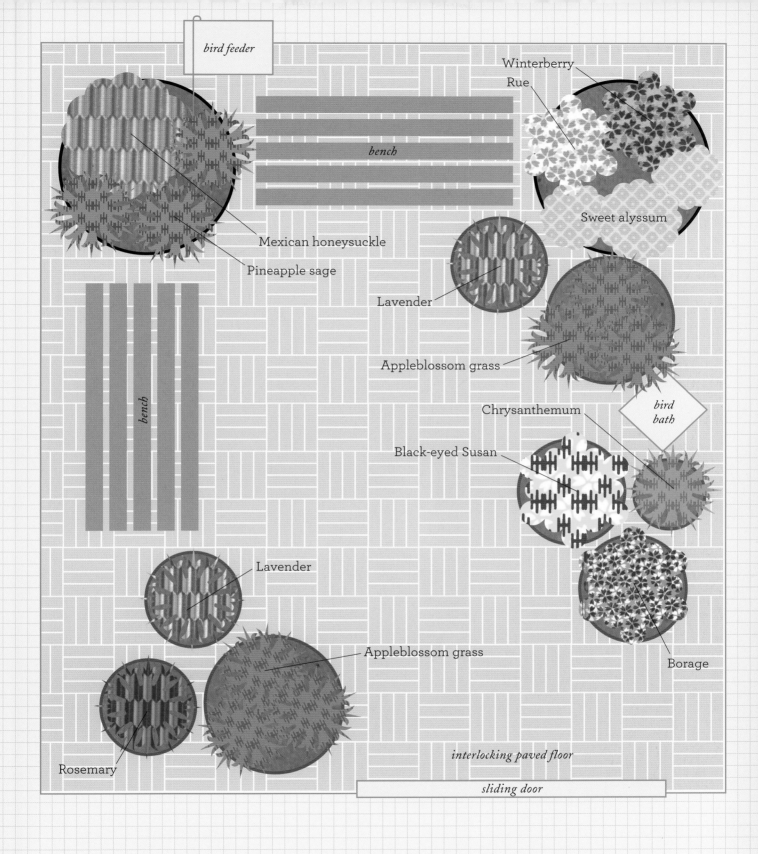

bird feeder

Winterberry
Rue

bench

Sweet alyssum

Mexican honeysuckle

Pineapple sage

Lavender

Appleblossom grass

bird
bath

Chrysanthemum

Black-eyed Susan

bench

Lavender

Appleblossom grass

Borage

Rosemary

interlocking paved floor

sliding door

POTAGER
WITH
A TWIST

Growing Gorgeous Food

A *POTAGER* IS A FRENCH-STYLE EDIBLE GARDEN that is as pleasing to the eye as it is useful. Especially attractive varieties of flowers, herbs, and vegetables are intermixed with one another and trained onto ornamental trellises instead of being grown in straight rows. It's like creating a beautiful flower bed except your blooms include ruby red chard and dangling purple long beans, vibrant orange nasturtiums and forest green zucchini, sprawling strawberries and blueberry hedges.

Taking inspiration from this garden style (putting the "pot" in potager, if you will) is a great way for gardeners on balconies, porches, and patios to have beauty and function, all rolled into one small space. Basic design principles, like thrillers, fillers, and spillers, translate easily to edible container gardens. Ruffled purple basil is a thriller to rival any ornamental plant, and herbs like thyme, prostrate rosemary, and oregano make delightful spillers. But don't stop there: choose beautiful pots that complement the shape and color of your edibles, and arrange them in pleasing compositions within the pot.

From edible flowers to vines and fruit trees to herbs, there are so many benefits to growing your own. The more you harvest, the less you'll have to spend at the grocery store, and the more certain you'll be that your food is organic. It is also so much fun, for children and adults alike, to try new foods when they are doused with that special ingredient called homegrown satisfaction.

Top: A container with strawberries dripping over the side is ideal for an ornamental edible garden.

Bottom: A view of the traditional potager gardens at the Château de Villandry in the Loire Valley, France.

Edible Flowers

A potager-inspired container combination.

It's much easier to grow your own edible flowers than to try to track them down to purchase. Take advantage of beautiful flowers that you can eat—the list is a lot longer than you might think. Edible flowers are quite versatile: slip them into a salad, dress up a drink, or just garnish a serving platter. As a general rule, it's best to harvest flowers in the morning.

Calendula (*Calendula* spp.). This wonderful annual flower can grow during the cool seasons of the year, or during the summer if it doesn't get very hot in your neck of the woods. My favorite, *C. officinalis* 'Zeolights', starts out bronze-orange and fades to light pink. If intense colors are more your style, you'll be able to find Crayola yellow and orange varieties. Use the mild-flavored flower petals to add color to salads or sweet batters, or to dye yarn or handmade paper. Plants grow to about 18 to 24 inches tall and are covered with flowers, so you'll have plenty of petals for culinary experiments.

Carnations (*Dianthus* spp.) have a sweet clove flavor that works really well for decorating desserts. Just be sure to remove the bitter white base of the petal before adding them to your edible creations. Tuck carnations around the base of other edibles—the 6- to 10-inch mounds won't compete with taller plants. Carnations are container-hardy in zones 4 to 8.

Daylilies (*Hemerocallis* spp.). With blooms that last only one day, daylilies are just the sort of frivolous that makes flowers fun. Try steaming the petals or unopened flowers with vegetables, or dipping opened flowers in tempura batter and frying

Nasturtiums flaunt gorgeous (and edible) blooms and lily pad leaves.

them. For all but the largest pots, you'll want to select miniature varieties of daylilies. My favorite daylily, 'Cinderella's Dark Side', has flowers so dark they're almost black. Some daylilies are container-hardy in zones 4 to 9, though most are only hardy to zone 6.

Marigolds (*Tagetes erecta, T. patula, and T. tenuifolia*). If you only have room for one edible flower, make it marigolds. I love mixing yellow, orange, and red marigold petals into wild rice for a festive side dish. And—when dried and crumbled—marigolds act as a poor-man's substitute for saffron. Marigold flowers also contain carotene, the same nutritious stuff that makes carrots good for you. The benefits of marigolds far surpass just looks and taste; their flowers attract beneficial insects to the garden; their roots give off a chemical that is to root-eating nematodes what garlic is to vampires; and their leaves and flowers produce a scent that is unappetizing to those insects that might like to chew the leaves of nearby plants. These annual plants form compact mounds ranging from 6 inches to 24 inches tall and wide.

Nasturtium (*Tropaeolum majus*) leaves and flowers have a nice, peppery kick: try them in a salad with baby spinach or sandwiched between bread slathered with cream cheese. You can even pickle the seeds if you're really adventurous. Choose from climbing nasturtiums (growing 4 feet or more) or tidy mounding varieties (18 inches tall and wide). Flower color ranges from the deepest mahogany to yellow, orange, and pink. I like *T. majus* 'Alaska' for its variegated leaves and brightly colored flowers.

GROW *more,* EAT *more*

The more growing space you can find, the more harvests you'll enjoy. Many garden catalogs carry plastic grow bags that have holes in the front where you can plant strawberries, leaf lettuces, herbs, and edible flowers. Hang these bags 6 inches apart on your balcony railings (assuming your landlord or homeowners association doesn't have a rule against this sort of thing). You can also experiment with hanging bags or buckets designed to grow vegetables upside down.

Raise taller plants off the ground by placing them on plant stands or benches (try cinder blocks and wood planks for makeshift benches) to create space for smaller vegetables, herbs, salad greens, and edible flowers. You could grow gigantic beefsteak tomato plants up top and window box varieties of cherry tomatoes like 'Tumbling Tom' and 'Bonsai' down below. A lot of herbs don't need much headroom either, like 'Greek Yevani' basil which has superb flavor and a surprising amount of leaves but only grows to about 6 inches high. If the upper shelf shades the lower space, choose from the many edible plants that tolerate, or even prefer, some shade:

❀Beans
❀Beets
❀Broccoli and cauliflower
❀Brussels sprouts
❀Catnip
❀Chamomile
❀Cilantro
❀Garlic
❀Kale

❀Mint
❀Nasturtiums
❀Parsley
❀Peas
❀Radishes
❀Salad greens
❀Swiss chard
❀Thyme

With plants on top of tables *and* below them, you can double the amount grown in one spot.

Hanging plastic grow bags are almost completely enveloped by edible greens and flowers.

Violas add whimsy to your salad bowl and a peppery zing to your taste buds.

Floribunda roses are characterized by the cluster of flowers topping each stem, and their nearly year-round flower display.

Roses (*Rosa* spp.). All miniature roses and most floribunda roses work well in containers. My favorite floribunda is 'Betty Boop'; other smallish floribunda roses such as 'Walking on Sunshine', 'Honey Perfume', or 'Day Breaker' are good choices too. Try cutting rose petals into long, thin strips and tossing them into your next fruit salad, or freeze tiny rosebuds in the center of ice cubes and add to lemonade or tea. When grown in a container, floribunda roses range in hardiness from warriors that can survive zone 5 winters to more delicate varieties that are only hardy to zone 7. Miniature roses are true garden rock stars that are container-hardy down to zone 5.

Sunflower (*Helianthus annuus*). Both the petals and seeds of sunflowers are edible. The petals have a distinctive bittersweet taste that complements mild lettuces nicely in salads. You can also eat the whole, unopened bud (prepare it like you would an artichoke). If you'd like to create a flowering privacy hedge, choose one of the tall varieties, like 'Mammoth Russian,' that can grow well over 6 feet tall. More diminutive varieties, like 'Sunspot', produce normal-sized flowers on 24-inch-tall stalks. Annual.

Violas and pansies (*Viola* spp.). Fresh or candied viola flowers are a wonderfully unique decoration for cakes and cupcakes. You can also toss them in salads for a mild pea flavor. Violas will quickly form a 6-inch tall mat, covering all bare soil. Select species are surprisingly hardy, sometimes reported as able to survive a zone 3 winter when grown in a pot. But most people treat them as annuals and replace them at least once a year.

Edible Vines

Inject beauty and height into your garden by training edible vines to climb up a decorative metal obelisk, or along balcony or porch railings to soften the edge of your space. If privacy is a concern, a few vines and a decorative trellis are in order.

Beans (*Phaseolus* spp.) are easy and inexpensive to grow from seed and several varieties display colorful pods and flowers. Look for 'Trionfo Violetto' pole bean (*P. vulgaris* 'Trionfo Violetto') or scarlet runner bean (*P. coccineus*). These beans will happily scramble up a 6 foot tall teepee trellis, providing height and privacy to your garden. You can expect tasty beans in about 75 days. Annual.

Cucumbers (*Cucumis sativus*). Note-worthy compact cucumber varieties include 'Spacemaster' (full-sized fruit on 3-foot-long vines), and 'Burpless Bush Hybrid' (6-inch-long cukes on 2-foot-long vines). Regular picking encourages cucumber plants to produce more prolifically throughout the season. Annual.

Hops (*Humulus lupulus*). If you'd like to try your hand at brewing your own beer, why not go all the way and grow your own hops too? Even if you're not ready to be your neighborhood brewmaster, these tough vines (container-hardy in zones 5 to 8) are a beautiful choice for covering as much as 20 to 25 feet of trellis, balcony railings, fence, or wall space. The light green female flowers, also called cones or strobiles, are very pretty against the dark green saw-toothed leaves.

Kiwis (*Actinidia* spp.) grow on attractive vines that thrive in part shade, often a challenging environment for edible gardeners. And did I mention that the leaves are splotched with green, cream, and magenta? Arctic kiwi (*A. kolomikta*) is hardy in zones 4 to 8 for container gardeners. You do need to plant both a male and female kiwi plant to get fruit.

Sugar snap peas (*Pisum sativum* 'Super Sugar Snap'). Give sugar snap peas a sturdy trellis or teepee and they will happily produce 5-foot-long vines that are heat tolerant and resistant to powdery mildew. About 60 days after planting you'll start to harvest delicious peas with crunchy, edible pods. Annual.

Scarlet runner beans (*Phaseolus coccineus*) growing up trellis for support.

Zucchini and miniature pumpkins (*Cucurbita pepo*). Ronde de Nice zucchini ('Baby Round') is a spectacular French heirloom that produces globular fruit in 3-foot-wide mounds about 60 days after planting. Wait to harvest until they are 2 inches in diameter but before they get much larger than 4 inches, or the flavor diminishes. Miniature pumpkins, such as 'Jack Be Little', do very well on a trellis and one plant will produce 5 to 10 palm-sized pumpkins about 90 to 100 days after planting. Annual.

Fruit Trees and Shrubs

Even small pomegranate topiaries will produce edible fruit.

If you need a shrub, hedge, or tree to complete your potager garden, why not plant one that has a nice shape, pretty flowers, and produces loads of edible berries? Blueberries are my favorite example of an edible hedge; currants and gooseberries are notable alternatives for shadier spaces. In warmer climates, upright forms of rosemary can easily be trained into a hedge with the advantage of giving off a wonderful scent when you brush past it.

Most fruit trees can be found in dwarf versions suitable for container growing but that are still large enough to add height and shade to your space. On my own balcony, I grow mandarins, peaches, nectarines, and figs; in the past I've grown apples, lemons, and blood oranges. When buying fruit trees to grow in a container, it is imperative that they are either genetic dwarfs or growing on dwarf rootstock. A genetic dwarf is a naturally short-statured tree (found most often in peach and nectarine trees); alternatively, and somewhat more common, are fruit trees grown on dwarf rootstock rather than their original roots. The top part of the young sapling is cut off from its original roots and spliced together with the roots of a different type of tree through a process called "grafting." The new roots give the tree some sort of benefit the original roots did not provide. In the case of container gardeners, the benefit we want is to transform the tree into a dwarf.

Apples waiting
patiently to ripen.

Apples (*Malus domestica*).
Readily available in dwarf sizes,
easy to train, and bearers of
delicious fruit, apple trees are a
great addition to any container
garden. If space is at a premium,
look for columnar apples such
as 'Golden Sentinal' or 'North
Pole' which will grow 7 to 9 feet
tall, but produce very short (only
a few inches long) side branches
called spurs. Container-hardy in
zones 5 to 9. In warmer climates,
choose apples that need very
few "chill hours" such as 'Anna'
or 'Beverly Hills', both of
which require only 150 to 250
hours of temperatures below
45 degrees F.

An apricot blossom is a
sure sign of spring.

Attractive foliage and tasty fruit make blueberries a gorgeous and useful hedge plant.

Apricots (*Prunus armeniaca*). I'm not sure which aspect of apricot trees is more delightful: the gorgeous flowers in early spring or the delicious apricots in mid-summer. The fruit of 'Tilton' tastes sublime whether fresh, frozen, dried, canned, or in baked goods; 'Harglow' is another great multipurpose variety. Hardy in zones 6 to 8 when grown in containers.

Blueberries (*Vaccinium corymbosum*). The best blueberries for container life are highbush varieties (as opposed to rabbiteye) that have been bred for short stature, commonly called "half-high." 'Bountiful Blue' and 'Sunshine Blue' are hardy in zones 6 to 10 and 5 to 10, respectively, and are both considered "midseason." Plant blueberry bushes in acidic soil and in containers that are at least 18 to 24 inches deep.

Blueberries produce fruit from late spring to late summer, depending on the variety. To get the best possible harvest, the flowers (which come before the berries) must be cross-pollinated with a nearby blueberry bush that is a different variety but is also flowering at that particular time of year.

This is less complicated than it sounds—all you need to do is find two different varieties of blueberry bushes that produce fruit at the same time of year. Your local bees will do the rest. Here are some other half-high blueberry cultivars that do well in containers:

❀ 'Northblue': large, wonderfully sweet berries, mid to late season.

❀ 'Northcountry': sweet, light blue berries, early to mid season.

❀ 'Northsky': a wild blueberry flavor, mid to late season.

❀ 'St. Cloud': large, flavorful berries, early season.

❀ 'Patriot': large, good-flavored berries, mid season.

Currants and gooseberries (*Ribes* spp.). Attractive currant shrubs (*R. rubrum* and *R. nigrum*), a great option for those with partial shade, will grow 3 to 5 feet tall. They are thornless and can produce white, black, or red marble-sized fruits. Gooseberries (*R. uva-crispa*) are closely related to currants. The sweet fruit ranges in color from dark red to pink to yellow-green and is perfect for pies and canning. Some gooseberries do have thorns so be sure to select a thornless variety, such as 'Friend'. Currants and gooseberries are both hardy in zones 4 to 8.

Culinary Herbs

Herbs present an especially easy opportunity to slip an attractive edible plant among ornamental plants to fill out the arrangement. I grow an incredible variegated form of thyme that has a heavenly lemon scent, and a ruffled, deep purple basil that easily holds its own in the beauty department. Likewise with sage: you have certainly seen the standard gray-green sage, but keep an eye out for the purple and variegated forms. They're just as useful in the kitchen, but add an extra oomph to the garden.

To combine multiple herbs (or any kind of plant, for that matter) in the same container, try pairing annuals with annuals, and perennials with perennials. That way, when the annuals are done, you can pull out all the plants at once and not risk damaging any of the perennial's roots. It may not always possible, but it's a good idea in principle.

These herbs all do particularly well in containers:

* **Basil** (*annual*)
* **Calendula** (*annual*)
* **Catnip** (*perennial*)
* **Chives** (*perennial*)
* **Cilantro** (*annual*)
* **Dill** (*annual*)
* **Lemon balm** (*perennial*)
* **Marjoram** (*tender perennial*)
* **Mint** (*perennial*)
* **Oregano** (*perennial*)
* **Parsley** (*perennial*)
* **Rosemary** (*perennial*)
* **Sage** (*perennial*)
* **Tarragon** (*perennial*)
* **Thyme** (*perennial*)

Many herbs, such as this purple basil, are beautiful as well as edible.

Look for unusual varieties of common herbs, like this variegated sage.

A collection of potted herbs
on a patio.

MINI BBQ
HERB GARDEN

Keep a container like this near your actual outdoor grill for easy flavor access. I planted Greek oregano (*Origanum vulgare*), French thyme (*Thymus vulgaris*), Thai basil (*Ocimum basilicum* 'Siam Queen'), chives (*Allium schoenoprasum*), and Texas tarragon (*Tagetes lucida*); you can pick whichever herbs suit your taste, just be sure to position the taller plants near the back and the trailing plants near the edges. The precise number of plants depends on the size of your BBQ and how full you like your containers. You won't need the grill grate or the lid, so if your BBQ is missing those it's perfect for this project.

SUPPLIES

1 portable BBQ or hibachi

1 coffee filter

1 small bag high-quality potting soil

3 to 5 herb plants

METHOD

1. Clean the BBQ, removing as much of the blackened grime as possible.

2. Place a coffee filter flat over the holes in the bottom of the grill. This will allow water to drain out but prevent the potting soil from falling through.

3. Fill up the BBQ with enough potting soil so that when the herbs are planted, they will be approximately 1 inch below the top edge.

4. Arrange your plants until you have a pleasing combination. Fill in around the plants with potting soil, gently tamping down as you go to make sure you get soil in all the nooks and crannies. Double-check the middle of a pot—I usually miss at least one spot there.

5. Place your BBQ in full to partial sun, depending on the needs of your herbs.

A recycled wine box is a great home for easy-to-grow greens.

Potager with a Twist Balcony

This contemporary balcony design includes a floribunda rose and gorgeous herbs flanked by two blueberry "hedges"—an homage to the traditional potager garden. Gain extra space in style with over-the-railing planters filled with fast-growing nasturtiums and hanging grow bags sheathed in strawberry foliage, flowers, and fruit. As the season progresses, swap the trellised peas and violas for runner beans and marigolds; and in the wine box planters, replace cold-hardy greens with loads of lettuce for summer salad days. A table centerpiece of potted lemon balm is a natural mosquito repellant so enjoyment of homegrown culinary creations can remain the primary focus.

COMMON NAME	SCIENTIFIC NAME	NUMBER OF PLANTS
Blueberries	*Vaccinium corymbosum* 'Sunshine Blue'	6
Floribunda rose	*Rosa* 'Betty Boop'	1
Lemon balm	*Melissa officinalis* 'Quedlinburger Niederliegende'	1
Marjoram	*Origanum majorana*	3
Nasturtiums	*Tropaeolum majus*	10
Salad greens	Various species	9
Super Sugar Snap	*Pisum sativum* 'Super Sugar Snap'	4
Strawberries	*Fragaria* spp.	9
Violas	*Viola* spp.	10
For grill:		
Greek oregano	*Origanum vulgare*	1
French thyme	*Thymus vulgaris*	1
Thai basil	*Ocimum basilicum* 'Siam Queen'	1
Chives	*Allium schoenoprasum*	1
Texas tarragon	*Tagetes lucida*	1

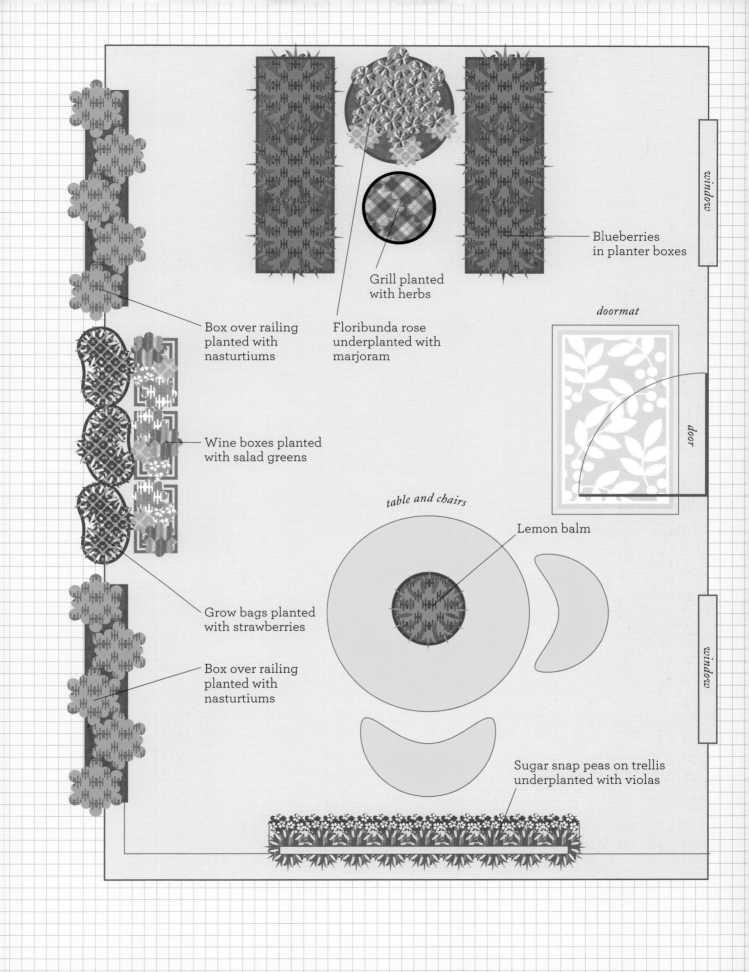

window

Blueberries
in planter boxes

doormat

door

Box over railing
planted with
nasturtiums

Grill planted
with herbs

Floribunda rose
underplanted with
marjoram

Wine boxes planted
with salad greens

table and chairs

Lemon balm

Grow bags planted
with strawberries

Box over railing
planted with
nasturtiums

window

Sugar snap peas on trellis
underplanted with violas

SUCCULENTS AND SCENTS PATH

Loving a Long and Narrow Space

IN THE DESERT SECTION of the Huntington Botanical Gardens in San Marino, California, a long strip of sidewalk is flanked by mixed borders overflowing with aeoniums, sedums, aloes, crassulas, and iceplants. The large swaths of vibrant colors—deep purple next to silvery-blue, alongside lime green and fire engine red—and the mix of tall and spiky plants with soft mounds of low-growing succulents, make for a visually stimulating succulent path. I always visit in the winter when the desert section is strutting its stuff and the bees are so heavily laden with bright orange aloe pollen that it's hard to believe their wings can still carry them from flower to flower.

It would be impossible to replicate the breadth of the Huntington in a container garden—after all, they need 10 acres to fit 5,000 varieties of plants—but that western walkway is the perfect inspiration for the long and narrow setup of many balconies. A space lined with succulents in all colors and shapes would make for a wonderful, albeit short, stroll through the garden. Intermingling fantastically fragrant flowers and dangling planted baskets among the succulents would take your pathway experience up another notch.

Red hot aloe flowers mark the beginning of a lovely succulent path in the Huntington Botanical Gardens.

Sculptural Succulents

The beauty of succulents is that their leaves are so colorful and interesting, that you almost don't care if they ever flower (which they do, freely and easily).

The huge diversity of size, shape, and color means that you could—and people definitely do—fill an entire garden with nothing but succulents. While some plants can brag about their long-bloom season, they still can't compete with aeoniums, sempervivums, and echeverias whose fleshy leaves look like flowers 365 days a year. And then there are crassulas, kalanchoe, and sedums that are shaped like tiny pagodas or jewelry chains. Who needs flowers when the plant itself is that interesting?

For a succulent pathway, it's nice to have a mix of thrillers, fillers, and spillers. Look to aeoniums, echeverias, and kalanchoe for the thriller role; find fillers in hens-and-chicks, stonecrop sedums, and stacked crassulas; and let burro's tail, string of pearls, and iceplants spill over the edges of pots. Most succulents need to be taken indoors during the winter if temperatures get close to (or below) freezing, but some hardier ones can withstand tough climates.

'Zwartkop' aeonium.

Aeoniums (*Aeonium* spp.). Dramatic burgundy *A. arboreum* 'Zwartkop' is a fabulous performer in a container garden; you can really set off the dark colors by placing a pot of silvery-leaved blue chalk fingers (*Senecio mandraliscae*) nearby. Over time, 'Zwartkop' will slowly grow to form a multibranched mound that is 48 inches tall and 24 inches wide. Hardy in zones 9 to 11.

Agaves (*Agave* spp.). Dwarf Utah century plant (*A. utahensis*) has thin, green, strappy leaves that grow in a tight bunch. Unlike some of the massive agaves out there, this one only gets to 10 inches tall and wide. Another relatively petite and hardy agave is variegated New Mexico century plant (*A. neomexicana* 'Sunspot') whose green and cream variegated leaves form a rosette that tops out at 12 inches tall and wide. Both plants are hardy in zones 6 to 10 when grown in containers.

Crassulas (*Crassula* spp.). Variegated jade plant (*C. ovata* 'Variegata') provides some zip, especially next to dark-leafed plants, as it grows very slowly to 48 inches tall or more. If it's red you desire, you absolutely must find the scorching *C. coccinea* 'Campfire', which forms a low-growing dense mat of red succulent leaves that look like mussels clinging to pier moorings. Both plants need to be taken inside for the winter in all zones except 10 and 11.

Dwarf poker plant (*Kniphofia hirsuta*). Add a splash of color to your scheme with the yellow and red flower spikes of *Kniphofia hirsuta* 'Fire Dance' which is among the shortest, prettiest, and cold-hardiest poker plants out there. Dwarf poker plant grows to about 18 inches tall and is container-hardy in zones 6 to 9.

Echeverias (*Echeveria* spp.). With so many variations and colors, there is truly an echeveria for everyone. A few of my favorites include loose and ruffled *E.* hybrid 'Compact Glow', pointy and modern *E. agavoides* 'Lipstick', silver fuzz-dusted *E.* 'Doris Taylor', and gorgeous plum-purple *E.* 'Perle Von Nurnberg'. Most echeverias are only hardy in zones 9 to 11, but a few, notably *E. subrigida*, are hardy to zone 8. Echeverias form ground-hugging rosettes; some plants are less than 6 inches tall, while others will grow to 18 inches or larger. Always check the plant tag.

Flapjacks (*Kalanchoe luciae*) has softly rounded, disk-shaped leaves that contrast nicely with spiky plants. The amount of sun exposure affects how much red blush the leaves exhibit. Gets to about 12 inches tall and is hardy in zones 10 and 11.

Hens-and-chicks (*Sempervivum* spp.). A prolific filler, each "mother hen" rosette will quickly be surrounded by her "chicks." All are under 6 inches tall and will spread out to cover whatever soil is available. The outer rosette of *S.* 'Black' is a beautiful purple-black with a bright green center; *S.* 'Red Rubin' is the exact opposite (deep red-black in the center and green around the edges of the rosette). *S. arachnoideum* has white fuzz that connects each tip of the rosette, making the plant look like it is covered in a spider's web. Most hens-and-chicks are container-hardy in zones 5 to 9.

Iceplant (*Delosperma* spp.) is funny common name for these South African natives. *D. ashtonii* 'Blut' is a great spiller that forms a mat of slightly flattened green leaves and deep magenta daisy-like flowers. Hardy in zones 6 to 9 when grown in a container. *D. congestum* 'Gold Nugget' is a trailing iceplant that will become completely covered with large yellow flowers; container-hardy in zones 5 to 9.

Stonecrops (*Sedum* spp.). Angelina stonecrop (*S. rupestre* 'Angelina') varies in color from chartreuse to yellow to orange, depending on how much sun, water, and rich soil it receives. Like many succulents (notably crassulas and aloes), pampering 'Angelina' will keep it green; stressing it with more heat, sun, cold, or nutrient-deficient soil than it wants will cause it to redden. I especially like using it as a groundcover in a pot in place of topdressing or mulch; eventually it will spill over the side of the pot, softening the edge. Another excellent choice is 'October Daphne' stonecrop (*S. sieboldii*) which puts on a glorious fall display of deep pink flowers and has beautiful gray-green foliage. Container-hardy in zones 4 to 10.

TIPS FOR *succulent* SHOPPING *and* CARE

Savvy succulent shoppers know that many nursery pots may contain several plants, not just one. It is often cheaper to buy a slightly larger pot of succulents with three or four plants in it than to buy four small pots of succulents with one plant per pot. Feel free to gently separate the plants and mix and match them. You can really keep your budget in check by using this trick.

When selecting succulents at the nursery, make sure the plants haven't been too battered. Customers grabbing for plants can scratch and permanently scar leaves, or knock them off completely (and those bygone leaves won't regenerate). While slightly damaged plants won't die from small scratches or a few missing leaves, it's good to be on the lookout for the best possible plant and handle carefully while planting. Also, many succulents have a silvery coating on their leaves that helps protect them from being burned by too much sun. When heavily manhandled, this coating will rub off; it will not regenerate so avoid purchasing plants in this condition.

Succulents are low-maintenance plants that require little pruning, fertilizing, and watering—great news because it means more time enjoying your plants and less time caring for them. That being said, no plant can be completely neglected, and part of the fun is giving them the TLC they need.

Be careful not to overwater succulents as they like soil to go almost dry between watering. The larger and fatter the succulent's leaves, the longer they can and should go without water. The goal is to keep the soil barely moist, just a hair before bone dry. Actively growing succulents (ones with new leaves or forming flower spikes) will need more water than the same succulent later in the season. Always water enough so that the water flows out of the pot's drainage holes to avoid salt build up in the soil.

Although succulents are accustomed to living in soil without many nutrients they do appreciate low-nitrogen fertilizer. It is easiest to add a liquid fertilizer to your watering can. Dilute it to quarter-strength and dole it out every four weeks during the third of the year the plants are actively growing. If your tap water tends to be hard, your plants will benefit from distilled white vinegar being added (at a ratio of 1 teaspoon per gallon) to their regular water. This will help acidify the soil and improve the efficiency of your succulents' roots in taking up nutrients.

The only necessary pruning is gently removing dead shriveled leaves, neatly snipping off flower spikes once they're done blooming, and cutting back and replanting rosettes when their stems get awkwardly long. Any branching succulent is potentially a source of cuttings than can be used to start new plants. Roots will form where leaves once were attached.

Echeveria runyonii 'Silver Onion'.

The Fragrant Factor

The flowers of chocolate daisy (*Berlandiera lyrata*).

How wonderful would it be to brush against a plant on your balcony stroll and release a flood of aroma? Consider perfuming your path with flowering plants that have scented leaves or fragrant flowers. Interestingly, many heavily scented flowers release their aromatic oils in the evening.

Chocolate daisy

(*Berlandiera lyrata*). If you like chocolate, check out chocolate daisy whose flowers—small and yellow with red-streaked undersides—smell exactly as you'd expect. To achieve a strong chocolate scent, grow several plants near one another. The scent is strongest in the morning and diminishes as the day warms up. Chocolate daisy will die down to the ground in winter and then pop up bigger and better than before, eventually getting to be about 18 inches high and 24 inches across. Container-hardy in zones 6 to 11.

Indian peace pipe

(*Nicotiana sylvestris*). The flowers of Indian peace pipe glow in the moonlight, dangling from tall (36- to 48-inch), airy stems: perfect for a narrow space that could use some vertical interest. Flowers are white, long, and tubular. Dozens of them dangle from the top of each stem. The effect, and scent, is wonderful. Annual.

Moonflower (*Ipomoea alba*).

Train moonflower to twine along your balcony or porch railings or up a trellis—you'll love the heart-shaped leaves and scented white flowers that unfurl in the evening. Unlike watching grass grow, you can actually see moonflower's blooms open up during a process that happens in just a couple of minutes at dusk. The vine can cover 10 to 20 feet. Annual.

Foliage of 'Chocolate Peppermint' pelargonium.

The trellis is doing double duty: supporting the star jasmine and providing a place to hang a few succulent pots.

Scented geraniums

(*Pelargonium* spp.). The fragrance of scented geraniums comes from their foliage (rather than the charming flowers) which means a wonderful reward every time you brush against them. Growers seem to be pretty obsessed with developing different scents—from lemon, cinnamon, and roses to peppermint, nutmeg, and ginger. Besides the aromatic qualities, many scented geraniums have particularly interesting foliage; the leaves of peppermint-scented geranium (*P. tomentosum*) are so heavily swathed in silvery fuzz that they resemble felt; skeleton rose scented geranium (*P. radens* 'Dr. Livingston') has beautiful soft green leaves that are deeply but delicately cut; and another rose-scented plant (*P. graveolens variegata*) has leaves flecked with creamy variegation and occasional soft pink flowers as a bonus.

Star jasmine

(*Trachelospermum jasminoides*) is an especially good plant for people who plan on spending evenings outside since the white flowers seem to glow in the moonlight, and the scent is often most fragrant at night. Although only container-hardy in zones 9 to 11, star jasmine can successfully survive a winter indoors if placed near a bright window. Winter jasmine (*Jasminum nudiflorum*) doesn't have that sexy jasmine scent, but it's hardy in zones 6 to 9 and has beautiful yellow flowers.

DESIGN *dos* FOR NARROW SPACES

Mirrors are a wonderful design trick for small spaces, especially narrow ones. For starters, they reflect light and a brighter space gives off happy, refreshing vibes. Additionally, by reflecting a beautiful image on what would otherwise be a blank wall, mirrors trick the eye into thinking the space is larger than it is. Even when you *know* that a garden is small, a mirror helps you feel less confined. For outdoor settings, it's best to use acrylic rather than glass mirrors. With that in mind, think creatively when looking for a mirror. A convex mirror meant to help drivers see around a blind corner or an old window frame from a salvage yard fitted with an outdoor mirror would add some character at the same time as it visually expands the space.

Lushly planted hanging baskets are a marvelous way to draw the eye upward—important in any garden, but especially one where you don't have width or floor space to spare. You can stick an iron shepherd's hook into the soil of one of your pots to hold the hanging basket (bonus points if the shepherd's hook has multiple hooks), or simply hang the basket from a decorative bracket screwed into the wall or a post. It's also nice to soften the hard lines of the shepherd's hook by training a vine to climb on it.

Putting interesting things to look at all along your balcony helps create an especially wonderful perspective from either end. Maybe your otherwise rather serious garden could use a boost in the whimsy department with a few mischievous garden gnomes. Or perhaps you have a collection of some sort that would be safe outside, tucked in and between pots. Of course, the occasional funky container set among the rest of your plants always injects some interest. After you've strolled along all those wonderfully interesting plants and garden ornaments, it's nice to have a destination, somewhere worth arriving that gives purpose to the path. Perhaps your destination is as simple as a charming table and chairs where you can sit with your chai latte and contemplate the meaning of life. It could be a particularly beautiful sculpture, fountain, or plant—like an exquisite bearded iris—just as long as it is special to you.

How's this for added height? A mirror also makes a narrow space seem wider.

Walking over to this table and chairs is such a pleasure thanks to the colorful collection of succulents along the way.

A hanging basket featuring string of bananas and a purple ruffled echeveria.

Hanging Basket All-Stars

'Pink Cascade' ivy leaf geranium.

Get the lush, dripping-with-gorgeousness look by selecting plants that thrill as they spill. For multiplant baskets, pair plants with similar watering and light needs.

Burro's tail

(*Sedum morganianum*). Pretty blue-green ropes of fat succulent leaves make for a great spiller that will trail up to 4 feet over the side of a hanging basket. Burro's tail is only hardy in zones 9 to 11, but happily overwinters next to a bright window inside.

Ground morning glory

(*Convolvulus mauritanicus*). Unlike other morning glories, the flowers of ground morning glory stay open all day. The blooms are either edged in cornflower blue, rosy pink, or white, with warm yellow throats. Ground morning glory forms a neat 12- to 24-inch mound spills beautifully over the side of a container or basket. The fast-drying nature of hanging baskets is perfect for ground morning glories (whose name provides a funny irony), as slightly dry conditions produce a better flower display. Annual.

Ivy leaf geraniums

(*Pelargonium peltatum*). This trailing type of pelargonium is a great choice for hanging baskets. A few of my favorite ivy leaf geraniums are 'Pink Cascade' (bubblegum-pink flowers), 'White Mesh' (pink flowers with white-veined leaves), and 'Black Magic' (deep burgundy-purple flowers).

String of bananas

(*Senecio radicans*). How can you not smile at a name like string of bananas? This easy-to-grow succulent spiller is outstanding for hanging baskets. The miniature-banana leaves offer great texture and contrast nicely with other succulents. While string of bananas is only hardy in zones 10 and 11, it will happily overwinter indoors near a bright window. The strings of leaves can get really long, up to 36 inches.

String of pearls

(*Senecio rowleyanus*). If you can master the slightly fussy water and light requirements of string of pearls—not too much, not too little—you'll be rewarded with 24-inch-long threads dotted with pea-like spheres. Occasionally the threads will burst into bloom with white, feathery explosions for flowers. Container-hardy in zones 9 to 11.

DIY HANGING BASKET

Some really neat hanging baskets are available these days, but if you can't find just the right one, it's easy to turn any lightweight container into a hanging basket. Pots that look like stone but are really fiberglass work well. As do various repurposed items, like decorative bundt pans or metal salad bowls. Just make sure to keep size in mind when choosing your vessel—you don't want to overburden your hook with a hanging pot that is extremely heavy because of all the soil and plants that are required to fill it.

SUPPLIES

1 lightweight pot

Length of string

Measuring tape

Drill

1 3-strand hanging basket chain set with hook

Potting soil

1 ivy leaf geranium (Pelargonium peltatum) *in a 1-gallon pot*

2 trailing plants in 4-inch pots, such as ground morning glory (Convolvulus mauritanicus)

METHOD

1. Wrap the string once around the pot, about a half inch below the top edge. Measure the amount of string that was needed to wrap around the pot. You now know the circumference of your pot.

2. Measure out a length of string that is one-third the circumference and use it to mark where to drill. Repeat this two times until you have marked three equally spaced holes (it's important that the holes are equidistant from one another so that the basket hangs level).

3. Drill the three holes and attach the chain to the pot. If your container doesn't already have a drainage hole, drill a fourth hole in the bottom of the container.

4. Partially fill the pot with soil. Place the geranium in the center of the pot, and a ground morning glory on either side. Fill in around the plants with potting soil.

The muse for this balcony garden
is the wonderful path of succulents
and the shabby chic urn at the
Huntington Botanical Gardens.

Succulents and Scents Balcony Path

Take a savory stroll past squat pots of fascinating and colorful succulents and hanging baskets dripping with plants, and end up at a cozy nook for two. The table and chairs are strategically positioned near a double-dose of scent—star jasmine underplanted with scented geraniums—the perfect place to while away a lovely evening. On the opposite side of the balcony, an antique birdbath planted with hardy sempervivums provides a visually balanced focal point. This design takes full advantage of the long and narrow setup that so often defines a balcony.

COMMON NAME	SCIENTIFIC NAME	NUMBER OF PLANTS
Aeonium	*Aeonium arboreum* 'Zwartkop'	2
Angelina stonecrop	*Sedum rupestre* 'Angelina'	8
Blue chalk fingers	*Senecio mandraliscae*	6
Burro's tail	*Sedum morganianum*	3
Dwarf poker plant	*Kniphofia hirsuta* 'Fire Dance'	1
Dwarf Utah agave	*Agave utahensis*	1
Echeveria	*Echeveria agavoides*	5
Flapjack	*Kalanchoe luciae*	3
Hens-and-chicks	*Sempervivum* spp.	14
Iceplant	*Delosperma* spp.	8
Indian peace pipe	*Nicotiana sylvestris*	1
Ivy leaf geranium	*Pelargonium peltatum*	6
Moonflower	*Ipomoea alba*	1
Scented geranium	*Pelargonium* spp.	6
Star jasmine	*Trachelospermum jasminoides*	1
Variegated New Mexico century plant	*Agave neomexicana* 'Sunspot'	1

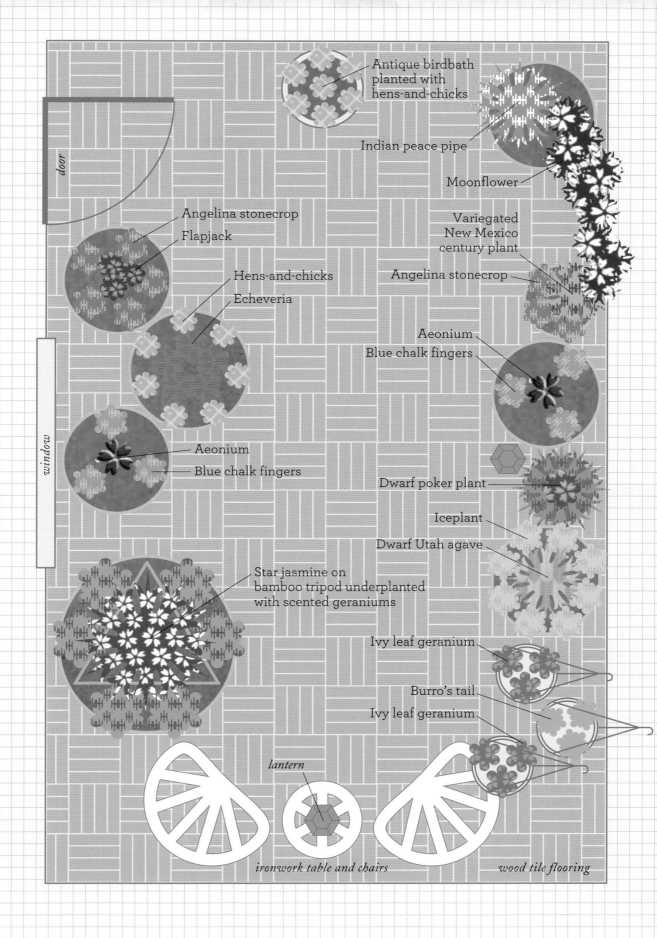

Antique birdbath
planted with
hens-and-chicks

Indian peace pipe

Moonflower

Angelina stonecrop

Flapjack

Hens-and-chicks

Echeveria

Variegated
New Mexico
century plant

Angelina stonecrop

Aeonium

Blue chalk fingers

Aeonium

Blue chalk fingers

Dwarf poker plant

Iceplant

Dwarf Utah agave

Star jasmine on
bamboo tripod underplanted
with scented geraniums

Ivy leaf geranium

Burro's tail

Ivy leaf geranium

door

window

lantern

ironwork table and chairs

wood tile flooring

THE SECRET GARDEN

Planning and Planting for Privacy

I LOVED THE BOOK *The Secret Garden* by Frances Hodgson Burnett when I was younger (still do, actually). The backdrop for the tale about friendship, renewal, and perseverance is a walled garden at Misselthwaite Manor, where an orphan named Mary lives with her uncle and disabled cousin, Colin, along with loving servants and talented gardeners. In the book, the children discover the secret garden and find walls covered with vines, overgrown rose bushes, crocuses, daffodils, butterflies, bees, and singing birds.

Wouldn't it be nice to have your own secret garden—a private, restful garden space in which to relax and rejuvenate? The challenge is that privacy, or rather, lack thereof, is an innate issue for exposed balconies (blame that on the mechanics of jutting out from a building) as well as patios and rooftops which often share breathing space with the neighbors. But with the help of some living privacy screens and potted trees—and a few non-planted ideas—you can create your own hidden world within a world. To add to the sense of being inside a jewel box, underplant the trees with flowering spillers.

Who wouldn't want their own secret hideaway?

Living Privacy Screens

A privacy screen made from a trellised *Euonymus*.

Most of the reasons why someone would consider adding a privacy screen to their garden are negative—perhaps due to a neighbor whose design ideas stop at "decaying sofa" and whose concept of great outdoor living involves incessant smoking and loud talking with friends—but privacy doesn't have to be just about excluding ugly views or annoying habits. You can redirect the focus to a beautiful row of lush shrubs, or a charming trellis and pretty vine.

When it comes to creating a privacy screen, planter boxes are the way to go. The long, deep boxes come in several different materials, including wood, plastic, and fiberglass. Several planter boxes lined up along the edge of your garden will help create a uniform look, and can provide more growing room for shrubs. Plus, they're frost hardy. I recommend either buying planter boxes with wheels or screwing on casters yourself, so that you can periodically rotate your boxes and help your plants get even amounts of light. Similarly, you can plant vines, such as bower vine, in a planter box and then train the vine up a trellis to provide privacy.

If the upstairs neighbor's balcony or the roof of a porch is directly overhead, keep the ceiling height of your space in mind when choosing plants. It might feel claustrophobic if you pick a plant that will grow to touch the ceiling. Remember to factor in how much the planter box is raised off the ground when determining the height of the mature plant. Also make certain to pick plants that match the amount of sunlight your space has to offer. Oftentimes people want to grow a living screen because the building next door is close enough to touch which means your space probably doesn't get full sun. And finally, select evergreen plants so you'll have year-round privacy.

Look for types of bower vine that have variegated leaves in addition to the typical red-throated pink flowers.

Bamboo. Some bamboos have gotten a bad name because they can take over through spreading rhizomes but that's not a concern for us container gardeners. Dwarf variegated bamboo (*Pleioblastus chino* 'Vaginatus Variegatus') has beautiful foliage, will grow to about 6 feet, and is hardy in zones 9 to 11. Consider broadleaf bamboo (*Sasa palmata*) for cooler climates or gardens without much sun; it's container-hardy in zones 7 to 10 and will reach about 6 feet.

Blue hibiscus

(*Alyogyne huegelii*). This evergreen shrub is related to tropical hibiscus (*Hibiscus rosa-sinensis*)—the plant we all think of when we hear "hibiscus." Not surprisingly, the flowers of blue hibiscus are like smaller, blue-lavender versions of the typical tropical hibiscus flowers. Blue hibiscus is a fast grower, so it's okay to buy a smaller plant if

that's all you can find or afford, within a season it will be 6 feet tall. Blue hibiscus is hardy in zones 10 and 11.

Bower vine (*Pandorea jasminoides*). I think the

prettiest variety of bower vine is 'Charisma'; its variegated leaves provide interest during the few months (spring through mid-summer) when the plant's red-throated pink flowers aren't blooming. Bower vine is only hardy in zones 9 and 10; if you need to replace it with a tougher vine, many varieties of honeysuckle (*Lonicera* spp.) are hardy down to zone 5 in containers, and cream pea vine (*Lathyrus ochroleucus*), native to much of northern North America, can even survive in a zone 3 container garden.

Gardenias (*Gardenia* spp.) are definitely up to the task of serving more than one purpose: a must for small spaces. Their glorious flowers smell divine and they have dark green glossy leaves that are easily maintained as privacy hedges. *G. augusta* 'August Beauty' will form a stellar privacy screen, as it grows to about 5 feet tall but doesn't spread out too much to the sides. Container-hardy in zones 9 to 11.

Heavenly bamboo

(*Nandina domestica*). Often planted on temple grounds in its native China as a symbol of good fortune, this is a lucky plant to include in any garden. While heavenly bamboo is not actually related to bamboo, its leaves do suggest bamboo leaves. Keep an eye out for more compact varieties such as 'Harbour Dwarf' or 'Firepower', but even full-sized nandinas top out at around 4 to 5 feet and provide ample privacy. 'Gulf Stream' is probably the most common full-sized variety, and displays the typical red-orange new growth. If you're looking for something more exotic, check out 'Plum Passion' whose new growth is a deep purplish red. Container-hardy in zones 7 to 9.

Podocarpus (*Podocarpus* spp.) is a lovely plant, as long as it isn't sheared into some sort of horrible shape. When left alone they form such nice, airy, well-behaved shrubs. Particularly beautiful, with its blue-silver leaves, is Icee Blue Yellow-Wood (*P. elongatus* 'Monmal'). Even in a container podocarpus can grow to 15 feet, but it responds very well to pruning so keep it at the height you want. Container-hardy in zones 10 and 11.

Blue hibiscus has charming flowers, and attractive, finely cut foliage that makes an airy privacy screen.

non-planted PRIVACY

Consider adding an umbrella to your garden space if the view you want to disappear is above you, or you want to screen out prying eyes coming from an upstairs window. Umbrellas give you a shady spot to relax, obstruct the unsightly view, and they don't scream "I'm trying to block out the neighbors." Dwarf umbrellas work well in smaller gardens; half umbrellas that sit flush with a wall are perfect for narrow spaces.

Pergolas are another great option for blocking out nosy neighbors that have the high ground. Since they're more substantial than an umbrella, pergolas tend to work best on patios that can be viewed by an upstairs neighbor. They add a bit of privacy all by themselves, but by training vines to grow on the pergola you can amp up both the beauty factor and its screening ability. Plop down a large pot next to each pergola post, plant a vine in each pot, and away you go.

Trellises, vines, flowering bushes, and small trees all combine to enclose this small patio and give it a sense of seclusion.

Underplanting with Style

Once your garden is cocooned in its privacy screen, it's nice to add dimension to the "walls" with small trees that are underplanted with lush spillers overflowing the pot. The spillers give the sense of an old world garden that has become charmingly overgrown. Be sure to take note of where any windows are so that you can put taller plants where you'll be able to enjoy them indoors—with the added benefit of a little extra privacy.

Abyssinian bananas add a sense of forbidden fruit to your secret garden.

Abyssinian bananas
(Ensete ventricosum) lend a jolt of color to your secret garden. This plant is best suited to warm climates like mine, but northern gardeners too will love the gigantic, red, tropical leaves—even if it means letting go of it at the end of the season. Try to purchase plants that were protected from strong winds and weren't knocked around too much, as their fronds are easily bruised and scarred from less than gentle care. Abyssinian bananas can grow to 10 feet tall in a container but they will stay much smaller when treated as an annual. Container-hardy in zones 9 to 11.

☀ Baby's tears (*Soleirolia soleirolii*) works really well in containers, quickly forming an airy, 4-inch mound that spills over the side of the pot and complements the lush, tropical feeling of abyssinian bananas. Treat as an annual in all but zones 10 and 11.

☀ Bacopa (*Sutera cordata*) is another hardworking annual spiller. It comes in white, pink, and blue-violet and can be purchased as a plant or grown from seed. 'Snowtopia' and 'Blutopia' are great varieties to try from seed.

☀ Trailing petunias (*Petunia* spp.) create glorious mounds that spill over the side of the pot. Some are so vigorous they'll start to pile onto the ground, which is a very pretty effect. To make sure that you're getting a trailing variety (as opposed to an upright petunias) look for ones in the Wave, Supertunia, or Surfinia lines of trailing petunias.

A winning contrast: 'Cherry Red' calibrachoa against the graphic black-and-white planter box.

Roses (*Rosa* spp.)—shaped through selective pruning and grafting into a "patio tree"—would be an amazing addition to a secret garden. People have been training roses into trees since at least the Victorian era, which is right around the same time that Burnett wrote *The Secret Garden*. Personally, I love how classy the all-white 'Iceberg' rose looks when it is trained as a standard. Some cold-hardy roses can survive a zone 5 winter in a pot.

Juniper (*Juniperus* spp.). Any secluded, formal garden would be well-served by a juniper trained into spiral topiary tree. Most varieties have two characteristics that make them especially apt for container gardening: they're slow growing, and only need a moderate amount of water. Junipers are pretty hardy and can withstand a zone 6 or 7 winter, depending on the variety.

❀ **Ground ivy** (*Glechoma hederacea*) is one tough plant. It will quickly cover any exposed soil and begin sending tendrils trailing over the side of the pot. The pretty leaves are scalloped and flecked with cream and soft green. Container-hardy in zones 4 to 10.

❀ **Carpet bugle** (*Ajuga reptans*) is a reliable, low-growing spiller that spreads by sending out runners; eventually it will arch nicely over the side of the pot. 'Burgundy Glow' has purple leaves with random white splotches, and spikes of bright purple flowers in spring and early summer. Container-hardy in zones 4 to 9.

❀ **Japanese sedge** (*Carex morrowii*) is a great option if you prefer the calm, contemplative look of foliage with few floral distractions. These plants look like grasses, with thin bladelike leaves that form a short, arching clump. Japanese sedge is container-hardy in zones 6 to 8.

❀ **Million bells** (*Calibrachoa* spp.) are the all-stars of the spiller flower world. You would be hard-pressed to find something negative to say about this annual plant: it comes in every color imaginable, it doesn't need deadheading, it's perky under all sorts of stressful conditions, it blooms nonstop from spring until first frost, it attracts hummingbirds, and on and on.

IN SEARCH OF
peace AND *quiet*

Apartment or condo life often means living *thisclose* to your neighbor and overhearing all sorts of things that you'd rather not. Or maybe your unfulfilled dreams involve having a conversation outside without broadcasting every detail to your neighbors. Living in a high-density area can also entail contending with noise from streets, trains, planes, jackhammers, and myriad other external noises outside of your control.

While utter peace and quiet may continue to elude those in close quarters, you can certainly find ways to reduce the noise or at least make it more bearable. Using two or three white noise sources at a low volume level—water fountains, wind chimes, radios, even a white noise machine—effectively diffuses background and unappealing noises and creates a more neutral sound environment. It's sort of a "can't beat 'em, join 'em" philosophy. If you don't have a power outlet that is easily accessible in your garden, keep an eye out for solar-powered fountains. As an added bonus, the birds your fountain is sure to attract may sing pretty songs that will either drown out your neighbors, or at least help you forget that they're there.

Listen to the pleasant sound of wind chimes rather than your neighbors' too-loud conversations.

FOUNTAIN OF TRANQUILITY

Fountains often bring to mind something of a grand scale—stone or marble perhaps—but even the smallest garden can have a water fountain. The great thing about this project is that it is not only a fountain but a container pond too. When planning, keep in mind that this project calls for an outdoor outlet to plug in the submersible pump (I've had success with both Smart Ponds and Laguna Ponds pumps). I planted golden variegated sweet flag (*Acorus gramineus* 'Ogon') in my fountain; other first-rate choices include:

❋ 'Baby Tut' umbrella grass (*Cyperus involucratus* 'Baby Tut')

❋ Calla lily (*Zantedeschia aethiopica*)

❋ Canna lily (*Canna* spp.)

❋ Corkscrew rush (*Juncus effusus* 'Spiralis')

❋ Elephant's ear (*Colocasia* spp.)

❋ Horsetail (*Equisetum hyemale*)

❋ Sweet flag (*Acorus calamus*)

SUPPLIES

1 small submersible fountain pump

1 container made from a nonporous material that does not have a drainage hole, approximately 24 inches in diameter

1 water or pond plant in nursery pot

2 to 3 cups pea gravel

Several bricks as needed

METHOD

1. Follow the manufacturer's instructions to configure the pump. Then cover all of the visible soil in the plant pot with gravel. Set aside both the plant and pump.

2. Place the container near an outdoor outlet. Stack enough bricks in the bottom of the container so that the plant and pump are at the right height: the pump's fountain attachment should be several inches above the water, while the top of the plant's pot should be 1 or 2 inches below the water. Put the plant and pump in place inside the container.

3. Drape the pump's electrical cord so that it snakes out of the pot near the back, hidden by the plant.

4. Fill the container with water up to just a few inches below the lip of the container. Plug the fountain pump in and enjoy the tinkling sound of water!

The Secret Garden Patio

Just being inside the tranquil cocoon of this patio, the weight of the world begins to melt away. Thick container plantings of bamboo, podocarpus, and mandevilla offer a sense of sanctuary even when neighbors are just steps away. Within the planted walls, delicate flowers spill over the sides of pots and a simple homemade fountain fills the air with a light splash of background noise. A comfortable set of table and chairs is essential to this relaxation oasis—go crazy with cushions and don't hesitate to put your feet up!

COMMON NAME	SCIENTIFIC NAME	NUMBER OF PLANTS
Abyssinian banana	*Ensete ventricosum*	1
Baby's tears	*Soleirolia soleirolii*	21
'Baby Tut' umbrella grass	*Cyperus involucratus* 'Baby Tut'	1
Bacopa	*Sutera cordata*	11
Corkscrew rush	*Juncus effusus* 'Spiralis'	2
Dwarf variegated bamboo	*Pleioblastus chino* 'Vaginatus Variegatus'	5
Gardenia	*Gardenia augusta* 'August Beauty'	1
Mandevilla	*Mandevilla* 'Sun Parasol Stars & Stripes'	3
Million bells	*Calibrachoa* spp.	5
Podocarpus	*Podocarpus elongatus* 'Monmal'	3

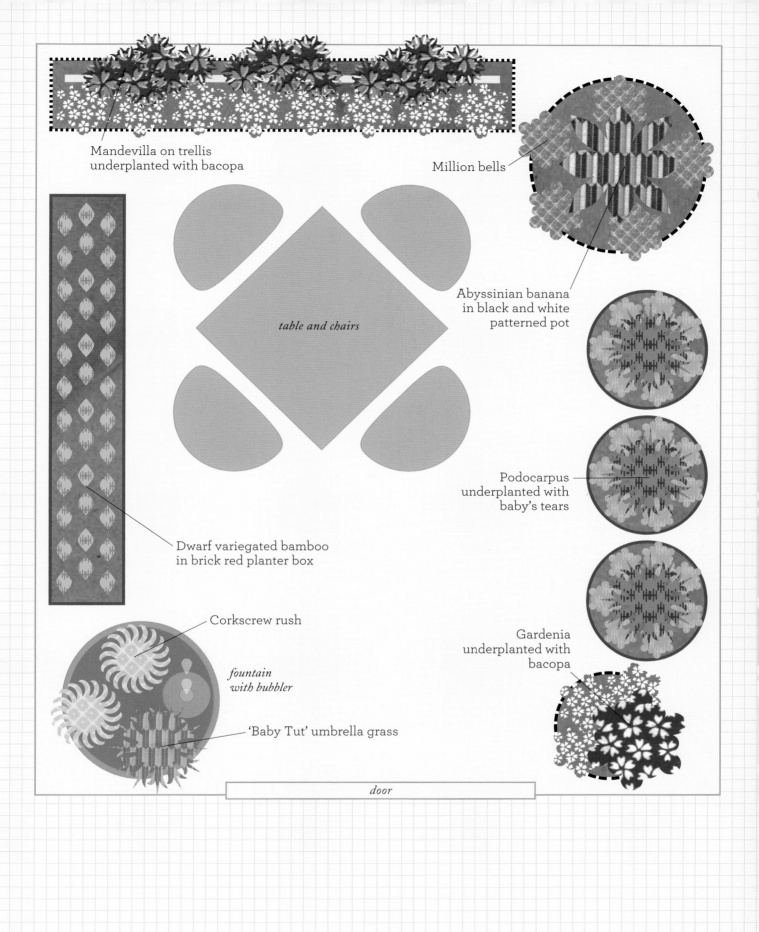

Mandevilla on trellis
underplanted with bacopa

Million bells

Abyssinian banana
in black and white
patterned pot

table and chairs

Dwarf variegated bamboo
in brick red planter box

Podocarpus
underplanted with
baby's tears

Corkscrew rush

*fountain
with bubbler*

Gardenia
underplanted with
bacopa

'Baby Tut' umbrella grass

door

VERDANT AND VERTICAL

Creating an Upward, Tropical Oasis

THE GREEN-HAIRED PARISIAN BOTANIST PATRICK BLANC started the craze for vertical gardens and is the creator of fabulously huge living walls in France, Italy, Spain, Poland, and India. His installation at Fondation Cartier in Paris looks as though a slice of the world's most luscious rainforest has been carefully hung, like a gigantic piece of art, above the front doors of the museum. Imagine tropical vines snaking their way down walls dripping with ferns, Japanese aralia, and hakone grasses. Emerging from the dense tropical undergrowth are actual trees—ficus and balsa to name a few—growing on a wall. The effect is stop-in-your-tracks stunning.

Tropically inspired vertical gardens—scaled down from Blanc proportions—are also breathtaking on balconies, patios, and porches. Get the lush look with tropical vines that meander the walls, arching ferns that spill out of soft-fabric wall planters, and bromeliads mounted on driftwood or hanging in the air. In other container gardens, you'd probably want an even mix of trailing and other sorts of plants, but overselect trailing plants for this garden. By expanding vertically, you'll gain more room to move around or sit down and enjoy a cup of coffee or a glass of wine, without sacrificing a single beautiful plant.

Draw the eye up with tall, narrow trees and a wall of planted Woolly Pockets.

Patrick Blanc's installation at Quai Branly Museum in Paris, France.

Bromeliads

The colorful, architectural forms of bromeliads—and especially tillandsias—are easy to love. In the wild, they grow clinging to trees, so it's only natural to mount them to the wall or plant them in a hanging basket or Woolly Pocket. Most bromeliads only bloom once, but they start creating new plants called "pups" off to the side which will eventually flower themselves. That being said, because you're only going to get one flower, you might as well pick a bromeliad with interesting foliage that has not sent up a flower spike yet.

Besides tillandsias, a few of my favorite bromeliads include *Cryptanthus* 'Black Mystic' which has black and white horizontal tiger stripes on its leaves, and *Neoregelia concentrica* 'Jeffrey Block' which has leaves striped lengthwise with white and green and a center that turns a bright magenta pink. Both of these bromeliads, and all bromeliads really, should be brought inside for the winter in all but zones 10 and 11.

Like bromeliads, succulents are amazing in vertical gardens. This display is at Flora Grubb's eponymous shop in San Francisco, California.

Airplants (*Tillandsia* spp.) are a really neat kind of bromeliad. They have no roots at all, and absorb all of the nutrients they need through their leaves, which are often silvery and corkscrew shaped. Who doesn't love a modern teardrop glass terrarium holding a funky little tillandsia? They look just as neat mounted on pieces of driftwood or simply displayed on a cake plate. Just promise me you won't hot glue a tillandsia to a magnet and put it on your fridge. Some tillandsias are also easy to get to flower, and often times their leaves will change to a bright color right before the plant flowers. Unfortunately, like all other bromeliads, once a tillandsia flowers, the plant will die, though they do make pups.

The level of hardiness varies greatly across the genus. Spanish moss (*Tillandsia usneoides*) is hardy in zones 7 to 11, while the intense red- and blue-flowered carnations of the air (*T. aeranthos*) can only stay outside year round in zones 10 and 11. During dry spells in between rain storms, water tillandsias by dunking the entire plant in a bowl filled with water 2 to 3 times a week. If you live in a very dry climate, mist your plants with a spray bottle in between dunking the plants.

A colorful bromeliad backed by lush green ferns.

Tillandsias growing in all their vertical beauty.

Ferns

Yes, my name really is Fern—it's on my birth certificate and everything! I once had someone insist that Fern was just my garden writer nom de plume. Believe me, I suffered with this name throughout my school years, I earned the right to use it now that it actually seems pretty cool. My name aside, I admit that ferns are a challenging plant for me to grow; they seem to like more humidity and moisture than I generally am able to provide. The upside is that you don't really know exactly how to care for a plant until you've killed it several times, making me an expert in fern care (at least that's my story and I'm sticking to it).

Many ferns are tropical and would meld seamlessly into a garden of bromeliads and tropical vines—and even if you select ferns that are more hardy than tropical, the lush green foliage should get the idea across.

A dramatic hanging staghorn fern draws the eye up.

The fronds of a Boston fern fan out on a steamy balcony in Austin, Texas.

A Tasmanian tree fern stands guard.

American maidenhair fern (*Adiantum pedatum*) has beautiful bright green, finely cut foliage. When grown in a hanging basket, the long fronds (up to 24 inches) eventually appear to completely envelop the container so it looks like a hanging ball of fern. Thanks to its eastern United States heritage, American maidenhair fern is container-hardy in zones 4 to 8. It may die back completely in the winter, but don't throw it out! The plant will reemerge when temperatures warm up.

Bear's paw fern (*Phlebodium aureum*) and **Boston fern** (*Nephrolepis exaltata*). Imagine the long, lobed fronds of bear's paw fern and Boston fern arching over the sides of a hanging basket or a Woolly Pocket wall planter. Both plants grow to about 24 inches tall and wide, and are hardy in zones 10 and 11.

Foxtail fern (*Asparagus densiflorus* 'Myersii') falls into the "not a true fern" category. This is all well and good because foxtail fern is much easier to grow than many true ferns while still adding architectural interest to containers. The closely related asparagus fern (*A. densiflorus* 'Sprengeri') also has long arching branches of leaves, but they are less tightly formed than foxtail fern. These faux ferns produce fronds that are about 18 inches tall and wide; hardy in zones 9 to 11.

Staghorn ferns (*Platycerium bifurcatum*) are a natural fit for vertical gardens since they grow attached to tree trunks in their native New Zealand and Australia. Replicate this original habitat by planting in a hanging basket or mounting the fern onto a piece of bark and then attaching that to a wall or another vertical surface. These plants truly have *presence*—the forked fronds resemble antlers, arching gracefully in every direction. With moderate water and partial shade, staghorn ferns will grow to 36 inches tall and wide. Bring plants inside when temperatures approach freezing, as they are only hardy in zones 10 and 11.

Tasmanian tree fern (*Dicksonia antarctica*). If your garden needs a little height and shade, look no further than Tasmanian tree ferns. They grow very slowly to 15 feet and have large, arching fronds between 3 and 6 feet long. Container-grown Tasmanian tree ferns are hardy in zones 10 and 11.

STEVE ASBELL'S *vertical* RAINFOREST

Steve Asbell is a young, apartment-dwelling newlywed who lives in humid, subtropical Jacksonville, Florida. The relatively mild winters and hot summers provide the perfect climate for Steve to grow his beloved orchids, bromeliads, and rainforest cacti. Though Steve has only considered himself a gardener for a few years, he has jumped in headfirst and already has an impressive vocabulary of botanical Latin and a blog about growing tropical plants outside the tropics (therainforestgarden.com). When you're hardcore like Steve, you say things like "I would eat in the garden more, but it's too easy to get distracted by all the plants!"

Steve particularly loves epiphytes—plants that cling to larger plants and trees in the wild rather than growing naturally in the ground—such as orchids and tillandsias. It's not surprising that Steve's balcony garden takes advantage of both horizontal as well as vertical space, considering that many of his favorite plants grow vertically in their natural habitat. He grows some plants in pots on shelves and a baker's rack, while others are mounted on driftwood or suspended in hanging baskets. Steve even made a piece of installation art by mounting a plastic frame filled with an epiphytic cactus (*Rhipsalis*) and orchids on the wall. His future plans include mounting all sorts of cool epiphytic plants on a rope hanging down from the ceiling.

Steve wasn't discouraged by the shady conditions on his north-facing balcony. In fact, he feels that a shady space is ideal since most of the plants that come from the rainforest grow underneath the canopy of very tall trees. Not all shade is the same, however, and Steve smartly arranges his plants to cater to specific light needs. Those that need brighter shade are placed higher up so they receive a bit of filtered light, while his plants that need very little light are closest to the ground where they get more shade.

Steve's Jacksonville balcony is home to so many tropical plants that he has had to make smart use of his vertical space.

Tropical plants arranged in a wall-mounted planter made out of a special soft fabric.

Vines for Tropical Flavor

An interesting old gate is a creative trellis for this gorgeous clematis.

Lush, dense rainforests are a hallmark of the tropics. The vigor and beauty of these vines will help you achieve that feel without losing valuable floor space.

Black-eyed Susan vine (*Thunbergia alata*). The common name of this plant is a telling clue as to its appearance. Much like the familiar black-eyed Susan (*Rudbeckia hirta*), the vine's flowers are usually yellow-orange with a black center. Some varieties have salmony pink, sangria red, or creamy white petals. Heart-shaped leaves round out an attractive vine that will grow to about 5 feet in a container. Black-eyed Susan vine is a fast-growing annual that is easy to start from seed. If you want to start it indoors, use a peat pot so that you can eventually plant outdoors without having to remove the pot; black-eyed Susan vine can be a little persnickety about having its roots disturbed.

Clematis (*Clematis* spp.) vines are some of the most adored in the gardening world—and for good reason. The breathtaking flowers can be found in a huge range of colors, shapes, and sizes. Many have a wonderful scent and most produce interesting seedpods. 'Arabella' is a wonderful, compact choice for containers. It only grows 6 feet tall but will be covered in violet flowers from summer to fall. Container-hardy in zones 5 to 8.

Mandevilla (*Mandevilla* spp.). You'll probably have a hard time choosing between the host of pretty mandevillas. These hard-working, shrubby, tropical vines bloom pretty much continuously from spring to first frost. Some mandevillas can grow to 15 feet or more under optimal conditions so be sure to pick a compact variety

The flowers of black-eyed Susan vine (*Thunbergia alata*).

Mandevillas will require you to secure them to the trellis, but their beautiful pink flowers are worth the effort.

if space is limited. Fashion a patriotic planting with 'Sun Parasol Stars & Stripes' which displays white streaks down each red petal, or just enjoy the unique variegated foliage of 'Pink Lemonade'. As the mandevilla grows, tie new growth gently to the trellis. Container-hardy in zones 10 and 11.

Passionflowers

(*Passiflora* spp.) have the most fascinating pistils and stamens that look as though they are going to start rotating like helicopter blades, helping the otherworldly flowers lift off and zip away. Pink passion vine (*P. sanguinolenta*) is a superb choice for container gardeners; its vines max out at 9 feet and the intense, coral-pink flowers are on display from spring through fall. If you live in the Southeastern United States, expect it to attract gulf fritillary butterflies and their bizarre-looking caterpillars. In other areas, keep an eye out for postman, red-spotted purple, and zebra heliconian butterflies. Container-hardy in zones 8 to 10, but will happily overwinter indoors.

Rex begonia vine

(*Cissus discolor*). The beautiful heart-shaped leaves of rex begonia vine are silvery-white with feathered green veins. It can grow quite long, spilling up to 10 feet down the side of a planter. Hardy only in zone 11, all other zones should bring rex begonia vine indoors whenever temperatures get close to 40 degrees F.

Pink passion vine (*Passiflora sanguinolenta*) is a great choice for containers.

VERTICAL PALLET GARDEN

Dumpster diving may sound unappetizing, but it's the best way to find a wooden shipping pallet that can be repurposed as a planter. I've had especially good pallet luck near the dumpsters behind supermarkets. No need to be squeamish—they're usually next to, not in, the trash bins. You might also try tracking down a pallet through Craigslist or contacting retail locations (like furniture stores) that receive goods on pallets.

Before you start, give your pallet a once-over: check for rotting boards, nail down any loose boards, and use sandpaper to smooth rough spots. This is also the time to decide which end of the pallet will be the bottom. You'll be covering the bottom, back, and sides with landscape fabric, leaving the front and top of the pallet uncovered. In the uncovered spaces, you'll be planting the flowers. I used linaria, nasturtiums, and lobelia; most small annuals sold in 6-packs would work.

SUPPLIES

Wooden shipping pallet

Hammer

Sandpaper

Small roll of landscape fabric

Scissors

Staple gun and staples

2 bags (4 cubic feet) potting soil

16 6-packs of annual flowers: two 6-packs per opening on the top of the pallet and one 6-pack per opening on the front of the pallet

METHOD

1. Lay the cleaned-up pallet face down and roll the landscape fabric over the back. Cut a piece of fabric that is several inches longer and wider than the pallet; the piece needs to be large enough to cover the back, bottom, and sides. Use the first piece of fabric as a guide to cut another piece that is exactly the same size.

2. Hold the two pieces of landscape fabric together as if they were one piece of fabric and center it at the top of the back of the pallet. Fold over an inch of the fabric and then staple into place near the top edge of the center of the top board. Smooth the fabric out to the left and right and pull it taut (it should be tight but not in danger of tearing). Staple the fabric down at the top edge of the left and right sides of the top board. Fill in between those staples with one staple every 2 inches.

3. Once the landscape fabric is securely attached at the top, smooth the fabric down and repeat the stapling process along the bottom edge of the bottom board; except this time, don't fold the fabric under—leave the excess fabric as a long flap.

4. Pull the flap of fabric tautly to cover the bottom of the pallet. Fold over an inch of the fabric and staple it down every 2 inches along the front edge of the bottom.

5. Now for the sides. Start at the bottom of one of the sides and fold the excess fabric inward as if you were wrapping a present. Then fold over an inch of the fabric and staple it in place near the front edge of the side. Smooth the fabric down and place a staple every 2 inches along the front edge of the side of the pallet until you reach the top. Repeat the stapling process on the other side of the pallet.

6. You should now have a pallet with landscape fabric covering the back, bottom, and sides. Add more staples along the back spine of the pallet and anywhere else that you think needs extra reinforcement. Remember: the fabric needs to be held down securely so that soil can't creep into places you don't want it to go.

7. Bring the pallet close to wherever its final spot will be and lay it down face up (the landscape fabric will be touching the ground). This is the position in which you will plant the pallet.

8. Unpot and slide two 6-packs of plants into each opening on the top of the pallet. Plant everything very tightly—you should have to practically shoehorn the last plant into place. After capping the top, pour an entire bag of potting soil onto the face of the pallet. Push the soil into the pallet between the slats and smooth it out so that the soil is level. Repeat with the second bag of potting soil.

9. Push potting soil into the bottom cavity of the pallet (directly below the lowest row of openings). Into this trench, plant one 6-pack per opening. The plants should be very tightly fitted into each opening. Next, push potting soil up against the flowers you just planted to make another trench beneath the second row of openings; plant one 6-pack per opening. Repeat this process for the remaining four rows of openings (two 6-packs per row).

10. Double-check that plants are completely covering every opening and there isn't any place for soil to fall out. Soil should also be firmly pushed into every part of the pallet where there aren't plants.

CARING FOR YOUR PALLET

Leave the planted pallet flat on the ground for a couple of weeks so the roots can start to grow in and hold all the plants in place. I must admit that I can never seem to wait—I always tip the pallet upright a few days after planting. When I do this, some soil does fall out although it always seems to be okay. However, it is better to do as I say not as I do: let the pallet settle for a few weeks before putting it in its upright position. Make sure to water your pallet regularly (they dry out quickly), paying special attention to the bottom two openings which seem to be the driest. Fertilize with water soluble fertilizer added to your watering can; follow package instructions for amount and frequency.

Verdant and Vertical Porch

This tropically inspired planting scheme turns shady porch into lush retreat with pots, hanging baskets, and soft modern wall planters filled with an assortment of ferns and bromeliads. While the overarching theme is definitely green green green, the flowering vine on the trellis and charming annual flowers in the repurposed shipping pallet add enticing pops of color. A row of tillandsias mounted on pieces of rustic driftwood evokes the epiphytic growth habits of these tropical rainforest natives. When temperatures dip, perk up your interior spaces with unique plants.

COMMON NAME	SCIENTIFIC NAME	NUMBER OF PLANTS
Airplants	*Tillandsia* spp.	4
Boston fern	*Nephrolepis exaltata*	2
Foxtail fern	*Asparagus densiflorus* 'Myersii'	2
Pink passion vine	*Passiflora sanguinolenta*	2
Staghorn fern	*Platycerium bifurcatum*	2
Tasmanian tree fern	*Dicksonia antarctica*	1
For Woolly Pockets:		
Bromeliads	Various spp.	1–2 per pocket
Ferns	Various spp.	1–2 per pocket
For pallet:		
Nasturtiums	*Tropaeolum majus*	5 6-packs
Verbena	*Verbena* spp.	5 6-packs
Sweet alyssum	*Lobularia maritima*	5 6-packs

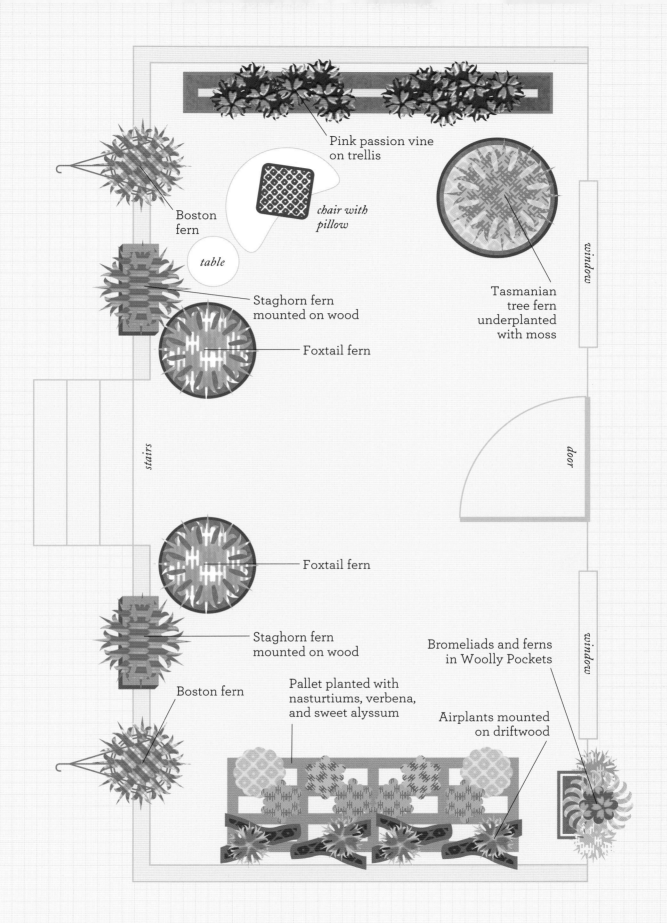

Pink passion vine
on trellis

chair with
pillow

Boston
fern

table

Staghorn fern
mounted on wood

Foxtail fern

Tasmanian
tree fern
underplanted
with moss

window

door

stairs

Foxtail fern

Staghorn fern
mounted on wood

Bromeliads and ferns
in Woolly Pockets

Boston fern

Pallet planted with
nasturtiums, verbena,
and sweet alyssum

Airplants mounted
on driftwood

window

GREEN THUMB CRASH COURSE

Learning the Essentials
for Success

A GREEN THUMB IS NOT HARD TO ACQUIRE, although you can't buy one at your garden center—you have to earn it. While it may seem overwhelming to read through all the steps required for proper plant care, just remember that these tasks are spread throughout the entire growing season. And when it comes time for maintenance, it's always a delight to be gardening on a 40-square-foot balcony instead of in a 400-square-foot yard.

The most important thing you can do to keep your plants alive and healthy is to look at them on a regular basis. Pretty simple! If a plant is still sitting in the plastic pot it was growing in at the nursery, then it's probably time to select the right kind of potting soil and find a more permanent container. If the plant looks wimpy or doesn't have a lot of flowers, you may need to take a closer look at your fertilizing habits. And if the plant is getting scraggly, it might need a bit of deadheading or pruning. Of course, every gardener makes a few goofs every year and the most valuable lessons are learned through trial and error. So chalk up any dead plants to the green thumb credentialing process and don't be too hard on yourself.

When taking care of your garden, a trowel and some canine company can both be quite helpful.

High-Quality Potting Soil

Cacti and succulents require a special kind of potting soil.

It's nice to talk about dynamite plant combinations or how to select the right pot. But if you don't use high-quality potting soil, those impeccably matched plants will be impeccably stunted. And a dead plant in a great pot isn't that sexy either.

The first thing to know is that you shouldn't use actual soil in your containers, and certainly never dirt from your yard. Garden soil carries pests, diseases, and weed seeds. Even brand-new bagged topsoil from the garden center is not properly formulated for the drainage that container-grown plants need. The stuff you want to use is called "potting soil," which is a misnomer because it doesn't contain any actual soil. For that reason, you may also see potting soil called "soilless mix." Manufacturers of high-quality potting soil are proud of their ingredients and happily brag about them on the bag. The mix will likely contain decomposed leaves and bark, perlite (those tiny white pebbles), peat moss (or coconut coir), and sand. Potting soil may also include additives to make the soil mix richer such as slow-release fertilizer, bat guano, worm castings, and lime. High-quality potting mixes will not be cheap but they are worth the money.

Make sure the potting soil you purchase is fluffy. If you can see or feel that the mix has formed hard clumps, put the bag back on the shelf. You should be able to squeeze the soil into a ball that will easily fall apart. The individual pieces that make up the soil should be relatively small; it should not resemble mulch.

SPECIALIZED SOILS

Generic potting soil will be just fine for most plants, however, some plants require a specialized kind of soil that mimics their natural habitat. Cacti and succulents, for example, come from arid regions with sandy or rocky soil. Almost all of them despise having "wet feet"—when their roots are in soggy, poorly drained soil. Regular potting soil is likely to keep things too moist for these fleshy-leafed plants so you'll want to look for specially formulated cacti and succulent potting soil.

Or, if you're feeling adventurous, ask local cacti aficionados for their potting soil recipe. They will probably suggest something along the lines of one-third coarse sand, one-third pumice, and one-third high-quality potting soil, but perhaps they will also divulge an extra secret ingredient. Palm and citrus trees both enjoy cacti and succulent potting soil as well.

Another thing you'll often see is a plant described as needing acidic or alkaline soil. This may sound mysterious, but it's not very difficult to figure out. The same idea in exists in the context of food: acidic foods are often described as sour (such as lemon juice) while alkaline foods are described as sweet (think watermelon). Acidity and alkalinity are polar opposites, and are measured on the 14-point pH scale, in which 0 is very acidic while 14 is very alkaline. Plants that thrive in part or full shade often prefer acidic soil because they have adapted to growing in a natural leaf litter mulch, and plant debris adds acid into the soil, among other good things. Other acid lovers come from regions with naturally acidic soil. Usually, plants that require acidic soil will be clearly marked as such on their plant tag. When in doubt, ask a nursery worker.

Why is all of this worth knowing? Because soil acidity or alkalinity directly affects plant growth. If you grow an acid lover in alkaline soil, it will not be able to take up nutrients. Same thing for an alkaline lover in acidic soil. While most people seem to like slightly sweeter foods, plants are just the opposite. Most plants like soil with a pH score of about 6.5. Camellias, azaleas, rhododendrons, gardenias, and blueberries are common examples of plants that like extra acidic soil, so you will often see a special soil blend just for them.

Potting and Planting

This a happy plant: it is planted at the right depth, it is getting the right amount of fertilizer, the mulch is helping keep the soil moist, and the gardener is being vigilant about watering.

This plant is potted too deep in the pot, which means it has less room to grow.

If you assemble a group of five seasoned gardeners and ask them how to pot a plant, you're likely to hear a couple different ways to accomplish the task. While there is always more than one way to do something right—in and out of the garden—certain ways of potting up a plant and caring for it are more likely to lead to a healthy, happy plant (and a proud gardener) than others. Paying attention to potting basics will save you a lot of future headaches because plants stressed by less-than-ideal growing conditions are more susceptible to pests and diseases.

DRAINAGE

Sometimes the simple things make all the difference. For example, it's really important to use pots with at least one drainage hole. If your desired pot doesn't have any way for water to drain out, you can always use a hammer and nail (for metal or plastic pots) or a drill with the appropriate bit (for all other kinds of pots) to make a hole or three.

If you use high-quality potting soil, the container should drain well on its own. I don't see any reason to fill the bottom of a pot with pebbles or any other foreign objects. Cheap potting soil can't be fixed by a layer of rocks—the bottom of the pot might drain well, but what about the layer of poor-quality potting soil that has compacted right above it?

On a similar note, please don't add packing peanuts to the bottom of large containers. I can't tell you how many times someone has shown me a plant that looks absolutely miserable and I later discover that packing peanuts have compressed into a giant plug, completely blocking the drainage holes. When water can't drain out of a pot, the soil becomes waterlogged and devoid of oxygen. Anaerobic bacteria multiply and things just get worse from there. In one such pot, the soil smelled so awful that I feel nauseated just thinking about it. If you want to reduce the amount of soil in a pot to make it lighter and easier to move around, or because your plant has a small root system, then use a pot insert to create a false bottom inside the pot. It's also a good idea to put pots in place before you plant them since they are easier to rearrange and maneuver when empty.

THREE *illustrated* STEPS TO *proper* POTTING

Fill the pot with enough soil so that when you place your largest plant into the pot, the base of the plant is about an inch below the top of the pot. Potting a plant too deep in the pot can reduce the amount of room the plant has to grow. Alternatively, potting the plant too high in the pot can make it hard to give the plant sufficient water. Tamp the soil gently to form a level surface. Place the largest plant (or the only plant, as the case may be) in the desired spot.

If the other plants you are placing in the same pot are in smaller nursery pots than the first plant, add enough soil so that the next largest plant's base will be level with the base of the first plant. Place that plant in the desired spot and repeat with all remaining plants. It's important to leave 1 or 2 inches between the soil line and the lip of the pot so that water can soak down into the soil and not run over the edge and out of the pot. The goal is to have a level soil surface in the pot, with all the plants potted at the same depth.

Fill in around your plants with more potting soil to eliminate gaps between the roots of plants. The roots of all plants should be completely covered. Be careful not to build up additional soil around the base of the plant; raising the soil line can cause several problems, including excess moisture that leads to rotting or infestations of insects and disease.

Rootbound? Re-Pot

If you can sneak a peek at the roots and you see roots that are circling the bottom of the pot, you've got yourself a rootbound plant.

If you don't repot your plants for years on end, the roots grow and expand so much that they take up all the space in the pot, or nearly all the space. The roots become a matted, tangled mass that cannot be separated without cutting the roots apart. If left in a rootbound state, the plant will eventually suffocate and die. Here are a few indicators that a plant might be rootbound:

☀The plant has stopped growing (the plant may still produce new leaves but no new shoots are forming).

☀Leaves wilt within a relatively short period after the plant is watered.

☀An inordinate number of leaves are dying and adjustments to the amount of water or fertilizer don't seem to help.

☀Roots are visible from drainage holes or in masses above the soil.

☀The top few inches of soil are impenetrable by your finger.

If you suspect that your plant is rootbound, the solution is to repot it. If you would like the plant to grow larger, plant it in a slightly bigger pot (perhaps 2 inches larger in diameter). If you don't want your plant to get much larger, then you can repot it in the same pot. Watering the rootbound plant deeply will help it slide out of the pot easier. Once the plant is out of the pot, remove all rotten and/or discolored roots. Trim back the roots by about one-third; then remove one-third of the leaves to balance the loss of roots with less demand from up top. Gently break up the remaining roots to help promote new growth. Put the plant in its new pot (or the thoroughly cleaned old pot) and plant in the routine way.

Newly repotted plants need a little extra attention. Because many of the root tips have been removed, the plant can't take up very much water. Put your newly repotted plant in the shade and mist daily, keeping the soil as wet as a wrung-out sponge. When you see new growth forming, you can return the plant to its old spot and regular watering schedule.

The Fertilizer Low Down

N-P-K numbers indicate what percent each element makes up in the total fertilizer.

All plants need certain naturally occurring chemical elements in order to grow. Carbon, hydrogen, and oxygen are derived from air and water, but plants also need macronutrients: nitrogen, phosphorus, and potassium (sometimes called "potash"). Nitrogen helps leaves turn green and grow faster. Phosphorous encourages root growth, disease resistance, seed and fruit set, and blooming. Potassium promotes drought- and disease-resistance, as well as root growth. Those three macronutrients are referred to as N-P-K, and you will see their percentages prominently displayed on all fertilizer packages, such as 4-5-2.

Knowing what each macronutrient accomplishes makes it much easier to select the appropriate fertilizer. It also helps that most fertilizers are pretty foolproof and state on the packaging what they're meant to do. For example if you are growing a flowering plant, choose "flower fertilizer" (which will have a higher second number than the first). Prepackaged formulations are available for all sorts of plants, from acid lovers to citrus to vegetables. Secondary nutrients (sulfur, calcium, and magnesium) and micronutrients (boron, cobalt, copper, iron, manganese, molybdenum, and zinc) are also important to the health of plants. However, most gardeners only pay attention to secondary and micronutrients when growing particularly tricky plants, or when a plant's disease is directly related to a nutrient deficiency.

TYPES OF FERTILIZER

Liquid fertilizers are the least disruptive way to fertilize your container garden. These fertilizers are meant to be diluted and then watered into the pot. To make life super easy, get a watering can with measurement markings on the side. Then all you have to do is put the right amount of fertilizer and water into the can and water your plants as usual. If the fertilizer you purchased only has instructions for traditional gardens, a good rule of thumb is to make the fertilizer half as strong and fertilize twice as often as the package recommends.

Another easy option that works well in container gardens is slow-release fertilizer. These small granules release fertilizer gradually, usually over a three-month period. Simply sprinkle some granules around the surface of the pot (the packaging will tell you how much) and water as you would normally. If you live in an area that gets tons of rain (say, Portland, Oregon), and your balcony or patio is exposed to the elements, the fertilizer will be released more quickly than it was designed to do. To solve this problem, use fewer granules than the package recommends and replace them more frequently, or experiment with a different type of fertilizer.

HOW MUCH?

To get things just right, think about what your plant needs and come up with a fertilizing plan. This is not as geeky and difficult as it may sound. It's a lot easier if you think in terms of what fertilizer is doing for your plants and what you want your plants to do. The idea is to fertilize plants when you want them to grow, produce flowers and fruit, and develop vigorous root systems—spring through early fall. You should cease fertilizing when seasonal changes start to signal to your plant that it is time to take a break (fall and winter). If you continue to fertilize too late in the season, your plant will produce new, tender leaves and flowers that will be damaged by the frosty weather of fall and winter.

To be a fertilizing wizard, you have to channel your inner Goldilocks. Too much fertilizer and you'll burn the leaves of your plants or cause the plant to grow too quickly and flop over. Leaves that are burnt from too much fertilizer look healthy, except for the edges, which are brown and look like they've been singed by a fire. Not attractive, and not good for your plant. On the other hand, too little fertilizer, and the plant's growth will be stunted: it may not flower or produce fruit to its full potential.

It's usually necessary to fertilize container-grown plants in a different manner than plants in a regular garden. When you fertilize a tree growing in the ground, the nutrients in the fertilizer are activated by water in the soil and move downward, which is fine because trees roots need to grow down too. But in a container garden, some of the nutrients are washed out of the pot with excess water and therefore are unavailable to plants. The way to rectify the problem of fertilizer washing out the bottom of the pot is to fertilize with a weaker solution, but more frequently. Giving the plant a weak solution of fertilizer on a recurrent basis mimics the amount of fertilizer in the soil of a traditional garden.

When and How to Water

Select shower-type nozzles for outdoor watering.

Some plants such as tree ferns and blueberries prefer their potting soil to be wet all the time. Others, like most succulents and cacti, prefer their soil to go nearly dry between waterings. Most plants are somewhere in between, and prefer soil that is moist, but not soggy. You can usually find all of this information on the plant tag or with a quick Google search.

Knowing how frequently a plant likes to be watered is only half the battle. You need a reliable way to tell whether or not the soil is still wet, has dried out a little, or is completely dry. The easiest way to do this is called the "two-knuckle test." Simply stick your finger in one of your pots until the first two knuckles are down in the soil. Wiggle your finger around. Does the soil feel really wet? Slightly moist? Bone dry? Use that information to decide whether or not that particular plant would like more water or is happy with the way things are. Whenever you water, gently sprinkle water evenly around the pot until you see water coming out the bottom. Then wait the right amount of time (conduct the two-knuckle test to confirm) before watering again.

I prefer using watering cans with shower nozzles since they don't wash the soil out of the pot or bash the plant. It's best to water in the early morning, if that fits into your schedule. Watering in the morning gives the sun a chance to dry up any water droplets that landed on leaves, reducing the likelihood of a moisture-loving disease afflicting your plant. Morning watering is less likely to disrupt beneficial insects (very few are active early in the day), and is also less conducive to building a hospitable environment for snails and slugs. During the height of summer you may need to water in both the morning and evening just to keep your plants hydrated and happy.

ALL OF THE *leaves* ON MY *plant* HAVE *wilted*—OH NO!

A common first reaction upon discovering that a plant has wilted may be running to find your watering can, but adding more water is not always the best thing to do. On particularly hot or windy days, even recently watered plants can sometimes look wilted because the plant is losing moisture through its leaves faster than it can take up water through its roots.

Stick your finger in the soil and check if it is still moist. If the soil has become hard and puckered to the point that it is pulling away from the sides of the pot, it's not enough to simply pour water into the container. In all likelihood, water will rush down the sides (in between the soil and the pot) and flow right out the bottom without wetting the soil. Try using a pencil to poke a few holes in the surface of the soil to allow water to penetrate in several spots. Add water until it flows out the bottom, wait ten minutes, and then repeat.

If the watering situation appears to be under control, move the pot to a lightly shaded spot. If the plant perks up by the time the weather cools down in the evening, then you know that the problem was the weather. If the plant in question can tolerate light shade, you might want to leave it there, at least during the heat of summer. Another option would be to move the pot to a location where it gets morning sun but is shaded in the heat of the afternoon. If those two things aren't possible, return the plant to its previous spot and continue to occasionally move it to the shade during heat waves.

If the plant still isn't perking up then it's possible that you overwatered the plant to the point that the roots have started to rot (often thanks to the *Phytophthora* fungus which loves super moist soil) and can no longer take up the water the plant needs. The plant may be beyond saving at this point, but certainly stop watering. Place the plant in part shade, and see if it recovers.

Get a Jump on the Season

If you live in an area with a short growing season, or are on a serious budget, you should definitely consider sowing seeds indoors while it is still winter. This effectively extends the growing season by starting with plants that are already several weeks old. And using packets of seeds will create numerous plants for a buck or two; trade extra seeds with friends (or make new friends by attending a seed-swapping event) to get more seeds for no money at all.

To get started you'll need a very bright window or a supplemental light. A standard issue CFL bulb is perfectly adequate if you are only starting a few plants inside. For starting a lot of seeds, you may want to invest in a shop light fixture and florescent tube light to get more even light over a larger area. You can purchase seed starting trays or make your own by poking a hole in the bottom of empty yogurt cups or other similarly sized food containers. As for soil, I've had more success with seed starting mix than regular potting soil. Seed starting mix stays evenly moist for longer periods of time, which is important for good germination rates.

To prevent damping off (a common fungus that can attack seedlings), keep a fan blowing very softly on your seedlings. The fan helps improve air circulation and will also strengthen the stems of your seedlings. Rotating your seedlings a quarter turn each day will also help make them strong. If seedlings are left to their own devices, they'll naturally stretch and grow toward the light source. Turning them tricks them into growing straight up.

WHEN TO START?

There's no hard and fast answer to the "when should I start my seeds" question. You'll first need to find out the last frost date for your area (the last day of winter or early spring on which you can reasonably expect to have temperatures at or below freezing). A variety of websites list last frost dates of major cities. Or consult a reliable expert, such as the folks at a good garden center or your county's master gardeners. Seed packets will tell you how many weeks before your last frost you should start those particular seeds. So if your packet says to start the seeds 6 weeks before your last frost, count back six weeks from that day and you have the indoor seed starting day for your seeds. Some plants will need to be started earlier than others, but expect most seeds to require 4 to 8 weeks of indoor growing.

Go even further with succession seed starting. Succession planting allows you to grow more plants in the same space by immediately planting a second crop when the first crop is finished. You can have your second crop waiting in the wings by starting those seeds indoors. For succession seed starting, count backwards from the expected maturity date of the first crop (instead of counting backwards from your last frost date). So, for example, if a seed packet says to sow the seeds indoors 4 to 6 weeks before your last frost, and your first crop takes 90 days to mature, start the second crop indoors 7 to 9 weeks after planting your first crop.

Nasturtium seedlings getting ready for spring planting.

FORCING BULBS IN FIVE EASY STEPS

Tulips, hyacinths, daffodils, and other spring-blooming bulbs will start appearing in your local garden center in late summer or early fall. This is because most bulbs need the chilly weather of winter to stimulate the development of a strong root system in order to bloom in spring. In cold climates, you can simply plant bulbs in the fall in frost-safe containers and leave them to their own devices over winter. But if you live in a milder climate, or you want to enjoy blooms indoors during winter, you have to force your bulbs—or trick them into thinking they've had a nice cold winter. Forcing bulbs is pretty simple and it can be done any place that provides consistent temperatures below 50 degrees F but above freezing temperatures, such as your refrigerator, garage, or basement.

SUPPLIES

Bulbs

Pot

Potting soil

Plastic bag

METHOD

1. Fill a clean, sterile pot with potting soil, almost all the way to the top. Put as many bulbs as you can in a single layer (for example, six tulip bulbs will fit in a 6-inch pot) and then nestle them in place, leaving only the pointy nose of the bulbs exposed.

2. Water the bulbs immediately upon planting; put the pot in a loosely tied plastic bag and place in the fridge or another cold spot.

3. Every week or so make sure the soil is still moist (water as needed) and check if roots are coming out of the drainage hole in the bottom of the pot. When you see roots sticking out and 2 to 3 inches of green shoots, it's time to bring the bulbs out of the fridge. Most bulbs require 5 to 6 weeks, but some, such as tulips, need as long as 16 weeks.

4. Place the pot in a cool location, such as a shaded corner of the balcony. Somewhere that is about 50 degrees F. Rotate the pot once a day so that the stems and leaves grow evenly and upright.

5. When the flower buds are plump and ready to open, put the pot in a sunny location, such as a bright windowsill or a place of honor on your balcony. Returning flowering plants to a cool location overnight will extend the life of their blooms.

These bulbs are ready to move into the fridge, where the cold temperature will signal them to start growing.

Daffodils (*Narcissus*) are easy to force indoors.

Deadheading:
Not for Deadheads

When I say you need to deadhead your plants, I am not suggesting that you turn them into hardcore Grateful Dead fans. What I mean is if there are dead flowers on your plant, it would behoove you to remove them. Pronto. Deadheading not only keeps your plants looking spiffy, it encourages them to flower again and again. Think about it from the plant's perspective. The plant strives to produce flowers that can then be pollinated by the wind, an insect, or a bird. Then, once the flowers have been pollinated, the plant can go about creating a seedpod which will eventually dry up and burst, spreading the plant's seeds all over the place. If you step in and remove the flowers before seeds have been created, you frustrate the plant's plan, and in an attempt to get itself back on track, it will often produce more flowers. If deadheaded, many plants will keep on producing new rounds of flowers all the way until they stop growing because of cold weather in the fall.

What's the proper way to foil your plant's seedy plans? If a plant produces relatively few, large flowers, simply use your clippers to cut the stem the flower is on just above the first set of leaves growing below the flower (or farther down the stem if you wish to shape the plant a little). If flower stems are soft, you don't even need clippers—simply pinch the stem between your fingers. For plants with a ton of small flowers, it is usually easier to just shear back the whole plant. Do this by cutting back the foliage by about two-thirds in early to mid summer.

Pinch the flower stalks off herbs as soon as they appear since flowers will diminish the taste of the leaves. The only exception is if you would like to save seeds for next year, in which case you'll have to let the plant flower.

WHEN IS DEADHEADING *NOT* A GOOD IDEA?

If you are growing a plant because you want to eat its fruit, then you do not want to deadhead. Remember, pollinated flowers turn into fruit. The fruit starts growing right behind the petals, so it is really hard to remove the flower without removing the baby fruit as well. Also, ignore what the Supreme Court wrote in *Nix v. Hedden*: tomatoes are not a vegetable, they are a fruit.

Another type of plant you don't need to deadhead are ones that have self-cleaning ornamental flowers, such as petunias, calibrachoa, and nemesia. The spent flowers will drop off on their own, which is basically the plant's way of telling you "I'm fabulously well behaved; I'll keep on blooming and looking nice without deadheading."

Basic Pruning Techniques

A lot of gardeners are scared of pruning, but there is no need to be intimidated. If you're just learning how to prune a particular plant, go slowly. You can always cut more, but you can never put a cut branch back. Well, technically there are some instances when you can, but I'm assuming you don't want to graft cut branches back onto the plant.

It's helpful to have a few basic principles in mind, regardless of what type of plant you want to prune. Almost all plants grow from the tips of their branches, not the base. If you cut the growing tip off of a branch, new branches will begin to grow from the sides of your cut. This will encourage a compact, bushy, full-looking plant. Another thing to understand—particularly for flowering and fruiting plants—is whether your plant blooms on twigs that grew this season

(new wood) or on twigs from last season (old wood). If you prune off the twigs from last season, and your plant blooms on one-year-old wood, you've cut off all the flower buds. Whoops! Just do a little research before you get clipping. And always make sure your pruning tools are clean (you don't want to give your plant any diseases while giving them a hair cut) and sharp (you want to make clean cuts).

Here's a quick guide to a few oft-grown container plants that require slightly more than baseline pruning care.

BERRY BUSHES

Lots of fruits with the word "berry" in their name are not actually berries, such as strawberries, which are—botanically speaking—an accessory fruit and require little to no pruning when grown in containers. The three true berries that are most often grown in containers are blueberries, currants, and gooseberries.

Blueberries need much less pruning than the closely related currants and gooseberries. For the first two years, blueberries need no pruning at all. Starting with the third year, and every year thereafter, completely remove the oldest, most scraggly looking branches. Also clip off any twigs that look weak. Cut back the remaining branches by a third to one-half. This relatively simple pruning will encourage your plants to make lots of new growth, which will produce better quality berries.

You can cut your bower vine back to just 12 to 18 inches tall and it will happily produce fresh, new growth.

An espaliered lemon tree
underplanted with marigolds.

Unlike most rose bushes, miniature roses do not need special pruning: just cut out dead growth and remove spent flowers and rose hips.

Currants and gooseberries, on the other hand, produce fruit on branches that are two and three years old. This means that a branch that forms in year one will not produce fruit. During years two and three it will produce fruit, and then in year four, the amount of fruit production will drop drastically. This means that you need to leave a branch on the plant for three years and then prune it off.

FRUIT TREES

Fruit tree shapes can be divided into two basic categories: central leader or open center (also called "vase"). Which you pick for your tree depends on the kind of tree you have. Apples, pears, and plums should be trained in the central leader shape. This means selecting a central trunk (the leader) and pruning off all horizontal branches except three or four main side branches. Peaches and nectarines should be shaped into the open center form, which means a short trunk with three or four evenly spaced branches trained to grow at a shallow angle from the trunk. Citrus trees don't need much pruning at all; you can allow them to grow free form or train them against a trellis for an espaliered look.

ROSES

Roses are tough cookies: it is extremely hard to kill a rose by pruning it too much, too little, or improperly. Pruning rose bushes—removing dead wood and shaping the plant—improves air circulation and encourages new growth and blooming. In mild climates the time to get started is midwinter, during dormancy. In climates where late frosts may damage new growth, wait until late winter or early spring, when small green buds have begun to form on the canes. Grab a pair of flower snips, good-quality bypass pruners, and some thick gloves. If you have a lot of roses, it might be worth buying gloves that cover your forearms all the way up to your elbows to avoid those gnarly thorns.

The goal for rose bushes (not groundcovers or miniature roses) is a vase shape, with four to six canes evenly spaced around the plant and an open center. Begin by removing all the leaves with the flower snips. This allows you to see the whole plant and get a sense of any problems you might want to correct. Then switch to your bypass pruners and cut off any dead canes, any suckers that are growing straight up from the soil, and any canes that cross each other or are growing into the center of the plant.

Next you'll want to focus on the remaining canes. Identify four to six canes to keep; they should be healthy, growing outwards, and evenly spaced around the plant. Remove any remaining canes that aren't one of the lucky four to six. Next, cut down the canes you are keeping so that they are between 1 to 2 feet tall. To decide where to make the cut on your keeper canes, look for swollen buds on the outside of the cane. Make an angled cut just above the bud, so that the pointy end is near the bud. Once you've finished this step you can pat yourself on the back—you're done.

THE UNINVITED GUESTS

Troubleshooting Pests and Diseases

WHEN PESTS ARRIVE IN YOUR CONTAINER GARDEN—and trust me, unless you live in a hermetically sealed biodome, they *will* arrive—it can be a real bummer. Sometimes they can do a lot of damage before you even notice that they've popped in to say hi. Make a habit of poking around in your plants regularly to see if you find any pests. It's also important to practice good gardening techniques since healthy, well-maintained plants are better able to withstand a pest onslaught than a plant that is barely holding on in the first place. And—you may not like this—if a plant happens to become severely infested, throw it out before the problem spreads.

When dealing with pests and diseases you have the opportunity to choose natural and organic methods of eradication. Besides the environmental benefits, keep in mind that avoiding broad-spectrum insecticides is the best method for preventing pest outbreaks since these insecticides tend to kill a pest's natural enemies, providing a clean slate for the pest to inhabit. The pests that you're most likely to come across in your container garden, at some point or another, are aphids, caterpillars, scale, snails and slugs, spider mites, and whiteflies. Keep reading for some tips on preventing their arrival and dealing with them if they still show up.

Beneficial syrphid flies look similar to bees except they don't have a stinger, you won't see pollen on their back legs, and they have only one set of wings.

Aphids tend to cluster together on soft, new growth.

A caterpillar enjoying the flavorful flowers of my Thai basil.

APHIDS

These tiny sap-sucking insects (in colors as varied as green, orange, and black) are often found in clusters on new plant growth or flowers. A single female can produce 50 to 100 offspring in her lifetime—and those offspring are ready to reproduce a week after birth—so you can see how quickly things can get out of hand. Young plants are most susceptible to irreparable damage from aphids so start plants indoors and protect them with a transparent barrier (such as a cloche or clear plastic tarp) when they are first moved outdoors. Heavy applications of nitrogen cause tons of weak new growth that aphids love so avoid overfertilizing with nitrogen. And work hard to keep ants off your balcony or patio since ants "farm" aphids, moving them from plant to plant and harvesting their honeydew secretions.

If you see just a few aphids, cut those leaves or twigs off the plant and throw them in the garbage. If the plant is sturdy (such as a rose) blast the aphids off with a strong spray of water. If you don't have easy access to a hose (or the plant is too delicate), just use a spray bottle.

Both adult and immature ladybugs are voracious eaters of aphids and other soft-bodied pests. The best way to use ladybugs to control your aphid population is to attract the locals by planting things that ladybugs love. If you can't seem to attract any local ladybugs, or you want the aphids gone yesterday, pick up a container of ladybugs at your local garden center. They aren't as good as the locals because they're often native to mountain areas and more likely to fly away. To reduce this problem, put the store-bought ladybugs in the fridge until late evening. This helps make them sluggish and more likely to stay the night. Sprinkle the ladybugs in all aphid-infested areas and hope they hunker down for the night and eat lots of aphids in the morning.

Insecticidal soap is an organic option that is great in situations where using natural controls, such as ladybugs, is not really possible. I've had a lot of success with insecticidal soap so I always keep a bottle in my potting shed (also known as a shelf in my garage). Make sure to spray plants thoroughly, covering both the tops and bottoms of the leaves to the point that they are dripping with the liquid. Wait at least a week before reapplying (and only if needed).

CATERPILLARS

My area of the world seems to be the international headquarters for cabbage loopers, which look like green inch worms but are actually the caterpillars of the white cabbage butterfly. Another common caterpillar pest is the appropriately named tomato hornworm, which has a gnarly spike on its backside. Nothing is more frustrating than pouring blood, sweat, and tears into your seedlings only to have a caterpillar chew them down to stubs. But at the same time, just as ugly ducklings grow into beautiful swans, ravenous caterpillars grow up to be beautiful butterflies. It's a tricky issue.

If you've had all you can handle of hornworms, cabbage loopers, and their friends, Bacillus Thuringiensis (Bt) is the answer. In a nutshell, Bt is a naturally occurring bacteria that is only toxic to caterpillars. Scientists have studied Bt extensively and found that it has no effect on humans, animals, other insects, or the environment; you can use it right up until the day of harvest on edible plants. Bt works by eliminating the caterpillar's appetite; they die of starvation within 2 to 3 days of ingesting leaves sprayed with Bt. To use Bt, spray an even mist on the top and bottom of the leaves of the affected plant. You want to thoroughly cover the plant, but not soak it to the point that the liquid is dripping off the leaves. I've never seen Bt at the big box stores, so you'll have to head over to your friendly independent garden center for a bottle.

A word to the wise: if you want to have butterflies, you have to tolerate the caterpillars. Planting flowers to attract butterflies, only to kill off all the caterpillars with Bt is the definition of shooting yourself in the foot. Moreover, Bt is an equal-opportunity caterpillar killer. You can't get rid of cabbage loopers without also eliminating Monarch butterfly caterpillars. In my opinion, it's only worth it to kill caterpillars if they are eating your edible plants. If they are doing their thing on ornamental plants, accept them as the price for enjoying butterflies' beauty.

Scale rarely gets so out of control that it damages the plant, but it is rather unsightly and can attract ants.

Some people think snails are cute. Not me. I don't think slimy tracks and mutilated leaves are charming in the slightest.

SCALE

If you absolutely had to have one pest, this is probably the most desirable one since scale populations generally stay pretty low and do little damage to the plant. It is, however, rather unsightly: immature scales and adult females look like small, flat bumps. Scale is found along stems, leaves, or fruit, happily sucking the sap out of your plant. Two basic types of scale exist: armored scale looks like tiny versions of barnacles stuck to the moorings of a pier or dock; soft scale can be smooth, cottony, or waxy, and is usually larger and more rounded than armored scale.

Scale produces honeydew, which attracts ants, which in turn protects the scale from natural predators and can lead to quick increases in scale populations. When scale gets out of control, it may cause leaves to look wilted, turn yellow, and fall off the plant. Fruit or twigs may also become deformed or blemished. Scale can be removed by gently rubbing a damp paper towel along the affected area of the plant, squishing and wiping away the insects. Insecticidal soap is a good back-up plan.

SNAILS AND SLUGS

Snails and slugs aren't usually a big problem for people who live high off the ground, unless you inadvertently bring them up there. More than once I've found the little buggers hanging out in nursery plants, so be sure to give new purchases the once-over before bringing them home. For those gardening on the ground floor, snails and slugs can be as annoying as they are gross. They leave their slimy tracks on the ground, pots, and plants. Not to mention that they munch on your baby greens like they are the best thing since sliced bread.

Snails and slugs, more active during cool evening hours, will be even further attracted to your plants if they are surrounded by a lot of super moist dirt and wet hardscape so it's best to water in the morning so you're not making it easy for them. Snails also like hanging out in plant debris so it helps to keep things clean.

If you have a real slug problem, try a product called Sluggo (made with iron phosphate, a naturally occurring mineral that is also used in fertilizers) which works similarly to Bt. Snails and slugs eat the pellets and then lose their appetite, eventually starving to death. Sluggo works best when soil

is moist, so apply in the evening after watering your plants. Scatter bait granules thinly and evenly (don't place it in piles) on the soil around or near the plants you want to protect. Sprinkle more granules two weeks later to catch any stragglers. Any Sluggo that is not eaten will harmlessly disintegrate into the soil.

SPIDER MITES

As much as spiders scare the living daylights out of me, I know that their presence is good for the garden. Spider mites, however, are a wholly different story. Although they are also part of the arachnid family, they are not a good kind of spider to find in your garden. Spider mites look like tiny moving dots amid small, dense webs. You're most likely to see them on the underside of leaves where they feed on your plants by sucking the sap out of the leaves. The leaves will then appear to have a smattering of light colored dots, before turning yellow and falling off. Spider mites really get going during hot weather—a limited problem can easily turn into a widespread infestation during summer.

Keep your plants well watered (water-stressed plants are the most likely to succumb to damage) and keep your hardscape swept since dusty conditions and lots of leaf litter provide ripe breeding grounds for spider mites (it looks nicer when things are tidy, right?). If spider mites are attacking a sturdy plant, spray them off with the hose. As always, avoid broad-spectrum insecticides; if you want to spray, use insecticidal soap or neem oil. To kill spider mites, the soap or oil must come in contact with the mite, so spray the affected area evenly, both on the upper and lower sides of the leaves. Never use soaps or oils on water-stressed plants or when temperatures get over 90 degrees F.

WHITEFLIES

Whiteflies look like tiny flecks of white cotton clustered on the undersides of leaves. Except unlike cotton, when the leaf is disturbed, they fly into the air in a tizzy, and then resettle on the leaf. Whiteflies harm plants by sucking their sap, which eventually causes leaves to yellow and fall off. Like aphids and scale, whiteflies excrete a clear, sticky substance called honeydew which can attract ants.

Spiders are infinitely more desirable garden visitors than spider mites.

There's no 100 percent effective way to treat large infestations of whitefly, so prevention is especially important. Outbreaks usually occur when a gardener uses a broad-spectrum insecticide that kills off whiteflies' natural enemies; when extremely dry, dusty conditions are present; or when a simultaneous infestation of ants are actively protecting the whitefly from its natural enemies (if you don't believe this is possible, check out the many videos on YouTube).

My mom is a vacuuming queen, so I'm dedicating this tip to her: if it's too late for prevention, bust out your hand-held vacuum to suck the adult whiteflies off infected plants. Vacuum in the early morning, when whiteflies are likely to be sluggish and easy to catch. Then wipe the leaves with a damp paper towel to remove whitefly pupae and nymphs from the plant. Be sure to seal the vacuum bag and paper towels tightly in a plastic bag and throw them out in a covered trash can—preferably far away from your container garden.

Planted Pest Control

Borage is one of many plants that you can use to attract beneficial insects—good bugs that eat pests and pollinate flowers.

There's no need for you to kill pests if you can convince beneficial insects—like ladybugs, bees, syrphid flies, green lacewings, and assassin bugs—to do the dirty work for you. These win-win plants are attractive to gardeners and beneficial insects alike:

❋ **Bachelor's buttons or cornflower** (*Centaurea cyanus*). This plant's extrafloral nectaries (a geeky way of saying the leaves release nectar even when the flowers are not blooming) attract bees, syrphid flies, ladybugs, lacewings, and beneficial wasps. Gardeners enjoy the edible blue or deep purple pom-pom flowers of this easy-to-grow annual.

❋ **Borage** (*Borago officinalis*). Aphid-eating green lacewings love laying their eggs on this plant. The hairy blue flowers of borage can also be candied or frozen inside of ice cubes for a splash of color.

❋ **Catnip** (*Nepeta cataria*). Scientists have determined that an essential oil in catnip attracts green lacewings. Since green lacewings eat aphids like they are the tastiest thing on the planet, this makes catnip an awesome companion for roses and other aphid-prone plants.

❋ **Dill** (*Anethum graveolens*). Harvest the leaves to season your culinary creations, but let the ladybugs enjoy dill's umbel-shaped flowers. Fennel (*Foeniculum vulgare*) is a similarly great plant both in the garden and the kitchen.

❋ **Sweet alyssum** (*Lobularia maritima*). Try growing sweet alyssum in between your edibles: it attracts bees (which are great for pollinating) and syrphid flies (which like eating aphids). Find the flowers of sweet alyssum in white, purple, yellow, or apricot.

❋ **Yarrow** (*Achillea filipendulina*) is another plant with umbelliferous flowers that beneficial insects like ladybugs love. Yellow is the most common flower color but also look for orange, pink, and red varieties.

Yarrow attracts lacewings, ladybugs, and syrphid flies.

Diseases

The most likely diseases that will affect your container garden are late blight, mildew, and mosaic virus. The majority of other diseases common in gardens are soil borne, and that's not an issue for container gardeners and their bagged potting soil. The line between problems caused by the gardener and those caused by diseases can be hard to find. Some human-caused problems look like diseases, and some plant diseases are primarily spread by things humans do, like smoking. It's good to know what these various problems look like so you can figure out the culprit and solve the problem.

LATE BLIGHT

The primary culprit behind the Irish potato famine back in 1845 was *Phytophthora infestans*, also known as late blight. This bad boy doesn't just attack potatoes; it also enjoys tomatoes, peppers, and eggplants (all biologically related members of the nightshade family). Late blight first appears on leaves as uneven, small, green, water-soaked spots surrounded by a zone of yellowish tissue. These spots expand quickly and turn into brown or purplish black spots that can be ringed by white spots (*Phytophthora* spores).

Avoid this problem by choosing varieties of potatoes, tomatoes, peppers, and eggplants that are known to be resistant to late blight (this information is usually loud and proud on the plant tag or seed packet), and always check for signs of late blight before bringing any plant from the nightshade family home. Preventative tactics include watering carefully so as not to splash excess water onto the plant's leaves, as well as spraying plants with compost tea. If your plant is infected with late blight, immediately bag it and throw it out. Wash your hands and any gardening tools that you used on that plant before returning to your container garden.

MILDEW

The two main types of mildew are caused by the exact opposite situation. Downy mildew requires water to be splashed on the leaves to move from leaf to leaf, and likes humidity above 90 percent. It appears as a fine, furry, grayish white-to-purple growth on the surface of older leaves (if you flip the leaf over, the area under the growth will be pale green or yellow). Powdery mildew, on the other hand, does not require moisture to spread and prefers mild temperatures and shade. It looks like powdered sugar has been sprinkled on the top and bottom of leaves. Some plant varieties have been specifically bred to be resistant to downy or powdery mildew; keep these in mind when purchasing plants.

If you already have a downy mildew problem, prune off infected branches as well as other uninfected branches to increase airflow through the plant. Also, avoid splashing water on the leaves of the plant when watering. Organic copper-based fungicide sprays can also help clear things up, just be sure to follow instructions carefully because some plants do not react well to copper sprays.

Try moving plants infected with powdery mildew to a sunny location and remove infected and excessive foliage to increase air flow through the branches. Avoid overfertilizing with nitrogen fertilizers (Miracle-Gro, for instance) because lush foliage creates the shade needed for the mildew to grow. If you caught powdery mildew early, fill a spray bottle with water and a few drops of dish soap and spray the leaves of the infected plant in the morning. You can also use neem oil to treat powdery mildew. As always, follow the package instructions and avoid using horticultural oils when temperatures are above 90 degrees F.

MOSAIC VIRUS

In container gardens, mosaic virus most commonly affects tomato, pepper, cucumber, petunia, snapdragon, and marigold plants. Mosaic virus often creates a random-looking pattern of dark and light green splotches, or a discoloration that appears as a light green zigzag throughout the leaves. It can be tricky to properly diagnose mosaic virus since plants with chlorosis (when the plant isn't producing enough chlorophyll) can look similar

A container plant can catch mosaic virus through insects, or if the gardener (or someone in the household) uses tobacco in any form. Tobacco is a common carrier of mosaic virus, and it is easily transferred to the user's hands, then to gardening tools and plant leaves. Most commercial greenhouses will not hire smokers for that reason. There is no effective method of curing mosaic virus, so you should focus on preventing it. If you smoke, or someone in your family does,

Downy mildew on boxleaf euonymus (*Euonymus japonicus*).

always thoroughly wash your hands before working with your plants. Tactfully direct guests to areas where they can smoke without endangering your garden. Clean your tools between pruning plants. And of course, try to avoid buying diseased plants, and look for plants bred to be resistant to mosaic virus. If you have an infected plant, immediately throw it out in a tightly sealed plastic bag, and wash your hands after handling the plant.

pesky PETS

Although this isn't a gardening practice per se, seriously consider keeping your cats indoors permanently. Scientists estimate in the United States alone, outdoor cats kill hundreds of millions of birds each year, and more than a billion (yes: billion with a b) small mammals. I have four cats, so please don't think that I don't love cats as much as the next crazy cat lady, but mine stay indoors at all times, for their safety as well as for the safety of neighborhood birds. If your pets do tend to roam free in your garden, here are a few tips to keep them from snacking on, or otherwise abusing, your beautiful plants.

❋ Distract cats' attention and fulfill their desire to eat plant material by giving them kitty grass, which helps aid their digestion. Likewise, be sure to take dogs on plenty of walks so they have access to grass to roll around in and eat, if so desired.

❋ I've noticed that my cats really like long, thin, dangling foliage, probably because it moves easily and looks like a fun toy. Stop the problem before it starts by avoiding plants that are particularly tempting to pets and by putting plants in out of the way places.

❋ Don't cover the soil in your pot with mulch or small gravel. Cats might think the material is a litter box and that scenario is so much worse than your cat eating the leaves.

❋ Spraying a solution called "Bitter Yuck!" on plants is often a successful pet deterrent. Originally developed to prevent animals from licking healing wounds, Bitter Yuck! is made with rosemary extract, which cats and dogs don't like. You can find this product at pet supply stores. Test an inconspicuous area of the plant first to confirm it won't damage your plant.

A container of lemon balm is a natural mosquito repellant with a much more refreshing scent than bug spray.

Plant Your Own Mosquito Repellent

Whenever I leave the arid Southwest, I'm always (painfully) reminded of just how many mosquitoes exist in the world. If you live in an area with a lot of mosquitoes, it may be pretty hard to enjoy your garden. Likewise, it's not fun to douse yourself in bug spray every time you want to enjoy an iced tea outdoors. But did you know that a plant can actually help you with this problem?

Lemon balm (*Melissa officinalis*) is a natural mosquito repellant. It has a very high level of a compound called citronellal in its leaves. Citronella—which is used in many commercial mosquito repellants—is the essential oil version of citronellal. Some varieties of lemon balm are up to 38 percent citronellal. The best mosquito repellant has a very hard to pronounce name: *M. officinalis* 'Quedlinburger Niederliegende'; it is hardy to zone 4, somewhat drought tolerant, and happiest with afternoon shade and soil on the dry side of moist. If you can't find it at your local garden center, you can buy seeds online; lemon balm is pretty easy to grow from seed.

When you want to activate your mosquito force field, simply pinch off a few leaves, crush them in your hand, and rub them over your skin. Feel free to pinch off leaves regularly as doing so will only encourage more growth. After all the work you've done, this last step toward making your garden a mosquito-free oasis is as simple as can be.

Conversion Tables and Plant Hardiness Zones

Length

inches	centimeters	in	cm	feet	meters	ft	m
⅛	0.3	7	18	¼	0.08	9	2.7
¼	0.6	8	20	⅓	0.1	10	3.0
⅜	0.9	9	23	½	0.15	12	3.6
½	1.25	10	25	1	0.3	15	4.5
⅝	1.6	12	30	1½	0.5	20	6.0
¾	1.9	15	38	2	0.6	25	7.5
1	2.5	18	45	2½	0.8	30	9.0
1½	3.8	20	50	3	0.9	35	10.5
2	5.0	24	60	4	1.2	40	12
3	7.5	30	75	5	1.5	45	13.5
4	10	32	80	6	1.8	50	15
5	12.5	36	90	7	2.1		
6	15	60	150	8	2.4		

Temperatures

$$°C = 5/9 \times (°F-32)$$
$$°F = (9/5 \times °C) + 32$$

Plant Hardiness Zones

Average Annual Minimum Temperature

ZONE	TEMPERATURE (DEG. F)	TEMPERATURE (DEG. C)
1	Below −50	Below −46
2	−50 to −40	−46 to −40
3	−40 to −30	−40 to −34
4	−30 to −20	−34 to −29
5	−20 to −10	−29 to −23
6	−10 to 20	−23 to −18
7	0 to 10	−18 to −12
8	10 to 20	−12 to −7
9	20 to 30	−7 to −1
10	30 to 40	−1 to 4
11	40 and above	4 and above

To see the U.S. Department of Agriculture Hardiness Zone Map, go to the U.S. National Arboretum site at http://www.usna.usda.gov/Hardzone/ushzmap.html.

Resources and
References

aHa Modern Living
www.ahamodernliving.com
A great site to check when you need a stylish garden tool, garden-inspired accessory, or gift.

Annie's Annuals
www.anniesannuals.com
A collection of interesting and hard-to-find plants from an independent nursery in Northern California.

Botanical Interests
www.botanicalinterests.com
A family business full of wonderful people and good quality seeds in beautiful and informative packets.

Bug Guide
www.bugguide.net
An easy to use website that will help you identify the helpful and not-so-helpful insects that are visiting your garden.

Floridata
www.floridata.com
An extensive plant database with detailed growing instructions.

Greenbo
www.greenbo.com.au
My favorite over-the-railing planter.

H. Potter
www.hpotter.com
A great resource for high-end pots and garden accessories.

The Lady Bird Johnson Wildflower Center
www.wildflower.org/collections
Find plants native to your area with this searchable database that sorts plants by state.

The National Wildlife Foundation
www.abnativeplants.com.
Website includes a native plant finder.

Seeds of Change
www.seedsofchange.com
If purchasing organic seeds and plants is important to you, then check out this seed company (everything they sell is certified organic).

Seeds of Diversity
www.seeds.ca
A great Canadian nonprofit dedicated to protecting heirloom plants of significance to Canada.

Seed Savers Exchange
www.seedsavers.org
Since 1975, this nonprofit has facilitated the exchange of approximately one million samples of rare garden seeds.

Territorial Seed Company
www.territorialseed.com
A good source for hard to find seeds and plants.

Books

Baldwin, Debra Lee. *Succulent Container Gardens: Design Eye-Catching Displays With 350 Easy-Care Plants*. Portland, Oregon: Timber Press, 2010.
A veritable bible when it comes to container gardening with succulents.

Chesman, Andrea. *The New Vegetarian Grill: 250 Flame-Kissed Recipes for Fresh, Inspired Meals*. Boston: Harvard Common Press, 2008.
Great recipes featuring vegetables (that you might have grown yourself) to grill out amongst your containers.

Crawford, Pamela. *Easy Container Gardens*. Canton, Georgia: Color Garden Publishing, 2008.
Container ideas using only tough, easy to care for plants.

Johnson, Catherine J., and Susan McDiarmid. *Welcoming Wildlife to the Garden: Creating Backyard and Balcony Habitats for Wildlife*. Seattle, Washington: Hartley and Marks Publishers, 2004.
Gardening and landscaping techniques lure birds, insects, reptiles, amphibians, and mammals to your yard or balcony.

McGee, Rose Marie Nichols, and Maggie Stuckey. *The Bountiful Container: Create Container Gardens of Vegetables, Herbs, Fruits, and Edible Flowers*. New York: Workman Publishing, 2002.
The go-to guide for growing edible plants in containers.

Rogers, Ray, and Rob Cardillo. *The Encyclopedia of Container Plants: More than 500 Outstanding Choices for Gardeners*. Portland, Oregon: Timber Press, 2010.
An excellent and beautifully photographed reference for container plants.

Sandbeck, Ellen. *Eat More Dirt: Diverting and Instructive Tips for Growing and Tending an Organic Garden*. New York: Broadway Books, 2003.
Accessible advice for those interested in organic gardening techniques.

Acknowledgments

I would like to thank Juree Sondker, my acquiring editor, for approaching me with the opportunity to write this book, for tolerating my procrastinating spirit, and for invaluable guidance while writing. Many thanks to Mollie Firestone, my project editor, for helping me rework, refine, and polish my ideas.

Without the love and support of my husband, Mickey, I would have never finished writing. Thank you so much for putting up with my neglected chores, insufficient attention, frazzled nerves, and for loving me all the same. Words can't describe how intensely grateful I am to have you in my life. I look forward to showing you for the next fifty years.

All of my family was very supportive. I am indebted to my parents, Rob and Roberta, for believing in me even when I didn't believe in myself, and to my brothers, Ben and David, for providing unconditional love and comic relief. My aunt Marilyn—a talented gardener herself—amazingly never tired of hearing about the book and encouraged me throughout the writing of it. I am also grateful to my uncle Rick, whose enthusiasm for photography is infectious, and who very generously contributed his photographs to this book. Thank you to Papa and all of my aunts, uncles, and cousins: you guys keep life interesting. I only wish I could have shared this book writing adventure with my Gramma, Grammie, and Grampie, especially since so many of my best memories take place in their gardens.

Finally, I would like to thank the community of talented garden writers I've been privileged to meet through blogging and the Garden Writers Association. When I was frustrated, you helped me keep my eye on the finish line. I look forward to the opportunity to return the favor.

Photography Credits

Index

About the Author

Fern Richardson is the voice behind *Life on the Balcony*, an award-winning blog devoted to gardening in tiny spaces and connecting container gardeners around the world. Fern's foray into gardening occurred in elementary school after receiving a book about creating wildlife habitats in urban areas. Luckily the resulting experiments, such as mosquito-infested manure tea, were not an indicator of future successes in the garden. Now a master gardener living in southern California, Fern grows herbs, peaches, nectarines, figs, blueberries, flowers, and succulents on a west-facing balcony and an east-facing front porch. Visit her at lifeonthebalcony.com.